# NURTURING OUR INNER SELVES

## A HUNA APPROACH TO WHOLENESS

Arlyn J. Macdonald

# NURTURING OUR INNER SELVES
## A Huna Approach to Wholeness
### Arlyn J. Macdonald

Using the extraordinary knowledge of the ancient priests, the kahuna of Hawaii, Arlyn J. Macdonald takes you on an intimate journey to self-discovery following the incredible development of the Self, or in this book, the Selves. Both the kahuna and modern psychologists agree that we are born with two minds or Selves: the emotional and the rational. We also have a third mind, a Higher Mind. Our Inner Family is composed of a parent and two children.

From the amazing perspective of the ancient knowledge of Huna, Macdonald shows how the Selves progress through the phases of human development from Prenatal to Elderhood to become integrated and whole. She discusses with clarity the skills of each phase and how we can return to a particular phase to reclaim mastery over skills we may have missed.

Nurturing our Inner Selves illustrates how the Mothering Principle and the Fathering Principle correlate to the emotional and rational Selves and how understanding these principles teaches us to be good parents to our Inner Selves. In becoming good nurturers we transform our lives and find a new wholeness.

Arlyn J. Macdonald is the author of *Inneractive Huna: a Guide to Self-Discovery Using the Teachings of the Ancient Hawaiians*. She is an ordained minister, international lecturer, and founder of the Inner Power and Light Company.

# NURTURING OUR INNER SELVES

## A HUNA APPROACH TO WHOLENESS

## Arlyn J. Macdonald

Inner Power & Light Company
Montrose, Colorado

*ISBN 0-7414-0398-6*

*Cover design by Christopher A. Master*
*Published by:*

*Infinity Publishing.com*
*519 West Lancaster Avenue*
*Haverford, PA 19041-1413*
*Info@buybooksontheweb.com*
*www.buybooksontheweb.com*
*Toll-free  (877) BUY BOOK*
*Local Phone (610) 520-2500*
*Fax  (610) 519-0261*

*Printed in the United States of America*
*Printed on Recycled Paper*
*Published April-2001*

Also by Arlyn J. Macdonald

Inneractive Huna: A Guide to Self-Discovery
Using the Teachings of the Ancient Hawaiians

Getting to Know You! An Introduction to Your
Subconscious Self Based on the Huna Teachings

Effective Huna Prayer

*This book is dedicated to our wonderful Inner Selves.*

# TABLE OF CONTENTS

# INTRODUCTION

To nurture is to love, nourish,
educate and train.

We are all nurturers and parents, whether we have offspring or not, for within each of us dwells two intertwining younger spirits or minds. These two minds or selves were known to the ancient *kahuna*, the priests of Hawaii, as the *'Unihipili* (Oo-nee-hee-**pee**-lee) and the *'Uhane* (Oo-**haw**-nay). The *kahuna* also knew of a third mind or self, the *'Aumakua* (Ah-oo-mah-**koo**-ah), who resides in the world of Spirit but is always connected to the other two selves by a golden cord of energy. The *'Aumakua* is our older and wiser mind, our Divine Parent. These three separate Selves or minds are united both molecularly and spiritually. They form the cohesive unit of consciousness of the Self. This is our Inner Family of a Mother/Father Parent, an older brother or sister, and a younger brother or sister. We are both parent and child on the inner level.

Modern psychologists name these parts of the Self, the subconscious mind, the conscious mind, and the superconscious mind, respectively. These are also known as the emotional mind, the rational or logical mind, and the spiritual mind. Scientists continue to search for the dynamic power that animates or brings life to the human being. The *kahuna* understood this dynamic power to be the living spirits of the *'Unihipili* and the *'Uhane* born into the physical body and the living spirit of the *'Aumakua* connecting them to the spiritual dimension. These three Selves together form the whole human being.

The ancient *kahuna* had a much better understanding of the psychological Self. To become a whole person they believed it was important to understand the characteristics of each Self and to establish a loving and trusting relationship of open communication between them. They also believed the spiritual world helped to integrate and sustain this wholeness. This is the art of nurturing in its highest form.

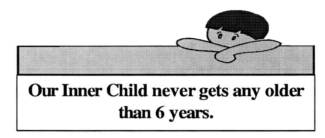

**Our Inner Child never gets any older than 6 years.**

The *kahuna* spent centuries carefully observing human life and discovered that each Self has certain characteristics and talents. Modern scientists are validating the findings of the ancient *kahuna* as the understanding of the human psyche grows. The emotional age of the *'Unihipili* is 3-6 years and **it never gets any older**, no matter the chronological age of the person. The *'Unihipili* is sometimes referred to as the Inner Child and it is always a child. The intellectual age of the *'Uhane* is 12-20 years and **it never gets any older**. The *'Uhane* is our older reasoning mind.

**Our Mind never gets any older than 20 years.**

The *'Aumakua* is ageless, since it resides in Spirit outside of time and space. The *'Aumakua* is our spiritual or Higher Self. It is defined as our "utterly trustworthy parental spirit," by Max Freedom Long, who recovered much of the ancient Hawaiian secret knowledge of the *kahuna*. Long termed this ancient knowledge *Huna*, which means "secret. Our Higher Self is our Holy Mother **and** Holy Father. The *kahuna* believed that this part of us has already learned how to be both mother and father. We draw on this wisdom to help nurture our other two Selves.

This book explores the phases of human development from the perspective of the *Huna* knowledge. We first learn about the characteristics of each Self and then study their growth through the various phases. We focus on the rapid development of the Infancy phase and see how the Selves learn the basic skills to master the world. We look at the traditional family values of the Hawaiian and how they apply to the modern family. We see how both the *'Unihipili* and *'Uhane* mature and grow through the phases of development from conception to death. We also explore the gender characteristics and energies of women and men in relationship to the characteristics and energies of the *'Unihipili* and *'Uhane*. We see how these characteristics shape our perspective on the world and our perspective on nurturing. We realize that each human must embrace the qualities of the female and the male to become whole human beings. We investigate good parenting skills for each phase of development and how to apply these skills to nurture and strengthen our Inner Selves. We learn how being a good parent prepares us for our new role as a Divine Parent, an *'Aumakua*.

Most of us have not mastered all of the skills of the developmental phases. We can use imagination, the wonderful talent of the *'Unihipili* and *'Uhane,* to return to the phase we have not yet mastered and recreate the proper circumstances and elements for learning those developmental skills. We use our imagination to recreate the ideal parental influence we needed at that age. The *'Unihipili* does not know the difference between fantasy and reality, so this is a great tool to use in accomplishing our task. We ask for the guidance and inspiration of our *'Aumakua* as we move forward toward new wholeness.

The techniques for reclaiming and mastering developmental skills are easy. The techniques include acknowledgement, forgiveness, reconstruction, ritual, experimentation and repetition. They require commitment, time and persistence. They also need the cooperation of both your *'Unihipili* and *'Uhane* and the guidance of your *'Aumakua*.

The information and theories contained in this book come from my research of human development and parenting, and my study of *Huna* for the past 30 years. They come from my own experiences in nurturing my Inner Selves. They also come from my experiences as a lay midwife and childbirth educator, mother of four children and grandmother of eleven grandchildren. And they come from the wisdom and inspiration of my Higher Self, my *'Aumakua*, my Divine Nurturer.

I believe the study of Huna offers a practical approach to wholeness. As you become more aware of the qualities, characteristics, and talents of each part of you, and learn how they progress through the phases of development, you will be able to nurture and love your Selves in a new way.

# THE THREE SELVES OF THE INNER FAMILY

"Our concern is to learn to understand our three selves, and how they can be made to work harmoniously together."
--Max Freedom Long

Our Inner Family is composed of three Selves, the emotional self or *'Unihipili*; the logical self or *'Uhane*; and the divine self, the *'Aumakua*. Max Freedom Long recovered the following characteristics of each Self after years of dedicated research into the ancient knowledge of the *kahuna*. The *kahuna* did not share their inner knowledge with those outside the priesthood, but used the knowledge to help their people. Much of this knowledge has been lost to the modern world, but what remains is invaluable for understanding our Inner Selves.

**CHARACTERISTICS OF THE *'UNIHIPILI***

1. It is a separate and conscious spirit.

2. It is a spirit that is connected to arms and legs.

3. It generates the emotions.

4. It is able to grieve and is the part of us that sheds tears.

5. It cannot talk.

6. It is something that covers up something else and hides it or is hidden by a cover or veil.

7. It is a spirit that accompanies another and is joined to it.

8. It is sticky or adheres to something.

9. It can attach itself to another and acts as its servant.

10. It does things secretly, silently and very carefully.

11. It does not do certain things because it is afraid of offending the gods.

12. It desires certain things most earnestly.

13. It is stubborn and unwilling.

14. It is disposed to refuse to do as it is told.

15. It can remember everything.

16. It has only elementary reasoning power.

17. It accepts and reacts to hypnotic suggestion.

18. It has a low voltage of vital force (*mana*).

The *'Unihipili* is the subconscious mind. It is the heart of our emotions and the storehouse of our memories. It is so closely intertwined with the conscious mind that the two are inseparable companions. It is secretive, stubborn and refuses to do what it is told. It has only elementary reasoning abilities. It is the wellspring of our emotions and sheds our tears. It cannot talk, but communicates through symbols, images, and feelings. It controls the senses and the extra sensory perceptions. It reacts to suggestions, especially hypnotic suggestions. It never sleeps, but remains always vigilant and in constant control of the bodily functions from conception to death. It has a low voltage of energy (*mana*), which it uses to keep the physical body functioning and healthy. It also shares this energy with the *'Uhane* and the *'Aumakua*. It is the younger brother or sister. It is a remarkable part of us that is to be respected, honored and, most of all, loved.

## CHARACTERISTICS OF THE 'UHANE

1. It is a separate and conscious spirit.

2. It is the spirit that talks.

3. It has the ability to use the power of words.

4. It is a pipe or channel for water (energy).

5. It is able to grieve.

6. It cannot remember a thought after it leaves its center of attention.

7. It uses inductive reasoning.

8. It cannot be hypnotized.

9. It is the part of us that sleeps.

10. It has the power to use Will of the hypnotic kind.

11. It is a guide or teacher.

12. It has a certain vital force of a medium voltage (*mana-mana*).

The *'Uhane* is our logical part, our conscious mind, that has the ability to use inductive reasoning. It talks and uses the power of words. It also has the ability to use the power of Will or intention. It understands all the emotions in their highest aspects, but does not <u>feel</u> these emotions. It is the older child, the guide and teacher of the *'Unihipili*. It depends on the younger Self for all memories, as it has no memory of its own. The *'Uhane* is the part of us that sleeps and travels nightly to the world of the dreamtime. It uses its medium voltage of energy, *mana-mana*, for the thinking process. It too is remarkable and is to be respected, honored and loved.

## CHARACTERISTICS OF THE 'AUMAKUA

1.  It is a separate and conscious spirit.

2.  It is a higher spirit or being.

3.  It is the older, entirely trustworthy parental self.

4.  It is attached to the body, but does not reside in it.

5.  It is the spirit that answers all prayers.

6.  It entwines as a vine.

7.  It has the power of creation and realization.

8.  It knows the past, the present, and the future that has already been crystallized.

9.  It can change the future.

10. It is the source of all healing.

11. It has a high voltage of vital force (*mana-loa*).

The *'Aumakua* is our Higher Self – both Holy Mother **and** Holy Father. It is our "utterly trustworthy parental spirit." It is that part of us that is connected to God. All prayers go first to our *'Aumakua*. It answers all prayers and works for our highest good, but we have to ask first. It dwells on the spiritual level but entwines the other two Selves on the physical level. It knows the past, present and future. It has the power to change our future by realizing our thoughts, wishes, desires and prayers. It has the incredible atom-splitting power of creation! It too is to be honored, respected and loved.

The connecting cord of energy flows between the *'Unihipili* and the *'Aumakua*. All communication between the *'Aumakua* and *'Unihipili* is nonverbal or symbolic and travels along this cord. There is no direct connection between the *'Uhane* and the *'Aumakua*. All prayers go from the *'Unihipili* to the *'Aumakua*. If the *'Unihipili* is not feeling worthy, it will hide its face away from the *'Aumakua* and will not send the prayers. There is a direct communication between the *'Uhane* and *'Unihipili* because they are so intertwined in the physical body. The emotional and logical centers of the brain interact on a very fundamental level. If the *'Unihipili* is not feeling loved or cared for by the *'Uhane*, it will not pass on any inspiration, intuition, or creativity it receives from the *'Aumakua*.

---

**Our Inner Family must be in a mutually loving relationship.**

---

It is critical then that the Three Selves have a mutually loving relationship. It is the responsibility of the *'Uhane* to be a guide and teacher to the younger, more inexperienced *'Unihipili*. The *'Uhane* must learn to gain the cooperation of the *'Unihipili* and not try to control the emotional Self through force. It is the responsibility of the *'Unihipili* to care for the physical body, share the *mana*, and send prayers. The *'Unihipili* must learn to control its wild emotions and become aware of the consequences of action in order to evolve to the next level of becoming a *'Uhane*. The *'Uhane* must learn higher thought, mediation, and good nurturing skills in order to evolve to the next level of Divine Parent. The *'Aumakua* must practice spiritual parenting, divine nurturing, and work for the highest good in order to evolve to its next spiritual level.

This is our Inner Family of Selves that needs to be nurtured, loved and cherished. As we learn to be good nurturers to our Selves, we learn to be good nurturers to our children and to others, for they too have an Inner Family.

**Inner Nurturing is based on love.**

# YOU AS A NURTURING PARENT

"Before you can become a parent, you must first become a whole person."

Traditionally, a parent is a nurturer, "one who brings up and cares for another, a source of origin. A parent is a mother or father of an offspring." (*The Merriam-Webster Dictionary*) Beyond that definition a parent is also a provider, a resource, a counselor, a teacher, a guide, an example, a role model, and a wellspring of love and energy. A parent is trustworthy, honest, fair, understanding, nonjudgmental, supportive, and a good listener.

The role of the traditional parent has changed in our modern society. Many children today have parents who are not their natural born mothers or fathers. The old American ideal of father, mother and the natural children living in their own house has little meaning in today's world. Families now consist of any combination of the following: one, two or three adults of the same or opposite sex; natural children; adopted children; step-children; foster children; and, grandparents and/or other relatives or friends. Single-parents raising children are either fathers or mothers. Both parents can be absent with grandparents taking on the parenting responsibilities. Older children are raising younger children.

Despite the change in composition, the idea of "family" still survives. This is because dwelling inside each of us is our Inner Family. A better definition of a family is "a symbol of qualities in close relationship to each other and attached to a single center." (*Dictionary of All Scriptures and Myths*) This definition describes the modern family and also our Inner Family. Each family consists of one or two adults in the parenting role and the children who are nurtured by them. Our Inner Family has a parent and two children.

What does it take to be a good parent and a good nurturer? James Hillman in his book, *The Soul's Code*, discusses the importance of being a person first, before taking on the role of a parent. He deplores the common assumption that being a parent is the most important thing in a person's life. He reminds us that before we can be anything else, we must first be ourselves. How do we become ourselves?

We become ourselves when we become aware of our Inner Journey. The most significant aspect of being a parent is our progress on the Inner Journey. This may seem like a strange place to begin. However, if we do not know who we are and where we are going, how can we hope to lead our Selves? If we do not know how to connect to our Divine Source for guidance and intuition, how can we teach our Selves? If we do not know how to generate, maintain and use our personal energy, how can we train our Selves? If we do not know our own Purpose, how can we affirm the importance of personal fulfillment for our Selves?

> **We are all going to the same place - HOME**

The Inner Journey is described in many ways. It is really the process of becoming a complete human being. We are all on this Journey. There are many roads, but only one destination – HOME. It doesn't matter which road you take to get there. In *Huna*, the Inner Journey can be described as the continuing process of understanding and communicating with your Three Selves. As you strengthen this ability you move towards wholeness and are directed to the fulfillment of your Purpose.

The first step on the Inner Journey is to take care of the physical body, for without a good vehicle for expression, we cannot function properly on earth. The 'Uhane helps take care of the body by providing a healthy diet, plenty of fresh water, and regular exercise for the 'Unihipili. The 'Unihipili is in charge of all the body systems, organs, glands and cells. On a cellular level our bodies also need energy or *mana*. *Mana* is generated by the 'Unihipili through the food we eat and the air we breath. *Mana* is present everywhere in the Universe and we can tap into this energy. We are at our physical, emotional, and mental best when we maintain a high level of *mana*.

The second step is to invite the spiritual into our life. In *Huna* we invite the Divine Parent, the 'Aumakua, to take its rightful place in the Inner Family. We must ask for Spirit to be a part of our lives before It will step in. We connect to our spiritual Self through daily meditation and prayer. We stay connected when we appreciate the wonder and beauty around us and see the Divine Presence in the faces of our fellow travelers. The third step is to discern our Purpose and then live our lives according to that Purpose. When we accomplish all of these steps we are on our way to becoming whole.

We are ourselves when we are whole. Carl Jung believed that our greatest urge is "toward psychological wholeness and self-actualization of our inner potential." Using *Huna*, both the goals of Hillman and Jung can be

> **We are ourselves when we are whole.**

achieved. We become a psychologically whole person and actualize our Selves through finding our inner potential, mastering the developmental skills, and living our Purpose.

Purpose is the urge to self-expression and is the motivation for our Inner Journey. It is the Inner Voice that called us here. Hillman calls it the *"daimon,"* the spirit of why we came. When we forget or neglect that spirit, that Purpose, we are no longer ourselves. The world has little meaning for us. Our *'Unihipili* becomes listless or restless, unfulfilled, or even angry when our *'Uhane* lets the monotony of daily living distract us from our Purpose. When we are working with our Purpose, our *"daimon,"* we feel happy and our lives have direction and energy. We are caught up in the flow of life. Being in the flow does not mean we don't have challenges. It means we feel alive, capable and positive, despite the challenges.

**Purpose is the urge to Self-Expression and motivates our actions.**

Mihaly Csikszentmihalyi has done a great deal of research on "flow." In *Finding Flow*, he says that to live does not mean biological survival. It means living in fullness, without wasting time and potential, "expressing one's uniqueness, yet participating intimately in the complexity of the universe." He goes on to explain that being in the flow is experienced when "what we wish and what we think are in harmony. It is the full involvement in flow, rather than in happiness that makes for excellence in life."

Csikszentmihalyi is using a *Huna* concept. When what we think and what we wish (feel) are experienced together, we are in harmony. When the *'Uhane* and *'Unihipili* are in concert, we move in harmony and become involved in the flow. Being in the flow means to respond to that inner call, living our lives as a direct action of our Purpose. Learning to stay in the flow is part of learning how to nurture the Inner Selves.

Another word for Purpose is "soul." G.T. Waters, author of *Follow Your Path*, expresses "soul" as the "Seed Of Unlimited Love." Our soul, he explains, is that part of us that is common to our Creator. Our soul talks to us in a quiet voice that always carries a consistent message. It is this message that is our Purpose for living.

Seed
Of
Unlimited
Love

Message is another way of describing our Purpose. James Redfield describes it by asking a question, "…what particular truth, unique to myself and my experience, can I now go out and convey to others about how one can live life more fully and spiritually?" In the *Celestine Vision: Living the New Spiritual Awareness*, he suggests we can discover our unique truth by looking at the lives of both our mother and father. What is the highest spiritual message of each parent? We can look through their eyes to understand their message. Our "challenge is to find a synthesis of our parents' perspectives, one that points to a more truthful existence." This synthesis is our Message. We synthesize and uplift the Purpose of our parents' lives.

> **What is your Message for the World? What is your Purpose?**

We instinctively know that we are born to Purpose. It yearns to be brought forth from inside of us. Our *'Unihipili* is the keeper of the knowledge of our Purpose for it was lodged in our heart before we were born. To become whole, we must bring this Purpose into our lives, nourish, support and express it. Our Purpose is what binds the Three Selves together as One. Our Purpose is always about bringing a deeper understanding of Spirit into the physical plane. As nurturing parents, we are to model our Purpose for **all** of our children.

Our earthly children are born to us to learn our Message. Our Message is a continuum handed down from one generation to the next. Redfield reminds us that "each generation, to whatever degree it is centered in spiritual thought, expands and evolves the world view of the previous one." Our grandchildren will refine this Message even more. It is part of our responsibility as parents to clarify our Message for our Inner Selves, so we can pass it on to our earthly children. Our Message is critical to the unfoldment of our lives. What message of Truth do you want to express through your life and pass on to the next generation?

> **Life is a continuum that flows from one generation, one level, to the next.**

Being a nurturer is also being a teacher. Your Inner Selves deserve to be taught everything they need to know in order to evolve. Teaching our Inner Selves includes teaching them about the physical world <u>and</u> the world of Spirit. They need to be taught that life is a constant, a continuum that flows onward from one generation to the next, from the physical to the spiritual and back again.

It is in learning how to nurture the Selves in the physical body that we prepare for the next stage in evolution. It is the *Huna* belief that life evolves from a lower level to a higher level. Each of us is a continuum of God. First we experience the mineral, plant, and lower animal kingdoms. Then we are born into the physical body as a *'Unihipili*, then a *'Uhane*, and then into the world of Spirit as an *'Aumakua*. Graduation for all of the Selves is simultaneous, when each Self has mastered the developmental skills and is ready for the next step. The *'Unihipili* becomes the *'Uhane* and the *'Uhane* becomes an *'Aumakua*. A new *'Unihipili* enters the physical realm from the lower animal kingdom. It is your continuum, your life constant. The *kahuna* believed that we return to another lifetime on earth if any one of the Selves is not ready for the next step.

Since the *'Aumakua* is both female and male, or directive and receptive energy, our Soul Mate becomes the other half of the new *'Aumakua* and the two continuums merge. The *kahuna* believed this merging continued on the spiritual plane with graduating *'Aumakua* evolving to higher levels until we evolve again into the consciousness of God.

Before you can become a parent, you must become a whole person. To become whole you must learn to honor your mind, heart, body and soul. You must maintain a high level of energy, stay connected to Spirit, follow your Purpose and enjoy Life. Only then can you begin to nurture your Inner Selves.

**FOLLOW YOUR PURPOSE**

# TRADITIONAL HAWAIIAN FAMILY VALUES

"We create ourselves and everything that comes into our lives.
– Traditional Hawaiian Teaching

The ancient Hawaiian culture has given us a great gift in the knowledge of the Three Selves. There is another Hawaiian gift that concerns family values. The values taught in traditional Hawaiian families are important values to teach our Inner Selves and our offspring.
In ancient Hawaii, every child was born in love and was welcomed and cared for by all the family. A description of the Hawaiian love for children is found in the book, *The Hawaiians*, written by Robert Goodman, Govan Daws, and Ed Sheehan. The book contains stories and descriptions of the life of the early Hawaiian people before Western and Eastern cultures became dominant.

A Hawaiian mother brought her child into the world upon an ancient birthing stone in a sacred place. This was the same place where her mother and father had been born. Life began at birth and life was respected and honored. All births in nature were honored, for all life is connected. The umbilical cord was symbolically cut to free the child for his own life. The *pili*, or navel string, was buried deep in a secure rock cavity protecting the personal power or *mana* of the child. The baby was carried home and fed by his mother's nourishing milk to strengthen him.

The mother molded the beauty of her child by massaging him with loving hands, "crooning a chant to his fine forehead, well-defined nose, long straight limbs, and shapely feet." She "sprinkled" him with love and when he grew older she buried him in the sand so his muscles would gain "power and form" from his struggling to get free. As the child grew he was

14

encouraged to share with the family, first carrying a small water gourd and then a smaller child. When he grew older, he was trained in the fields that interested him and for which he had the most talent. When children came of age, they were taught "the loveliness of making beautiful children of their own."

The Hawaiians believed that life is a "precious state and should be filled with beauty, joy and love, with courtesy and generosity." These beliefs were taught to the children. Everything was shared, even troubles. If a member of the family became ill in mind, body, or spirit, it was the concern of the entire family. The family gathered and "made things right," by talking out the problem, resolving any hurts, and taking action. Children grew up knowing that what effects one effects all.

> **The Elders were respected and honored.**

The aged and senile were cared for, respected and honored, for they were the ones "who first loved us." No one told a person when to be an elder. It was up to the individual to decide when he or she could no longer work. Many older people were productive members of the family up until their deaths.

There were no orphans and few childless couples. Children were shared by those parents who were blessed with many. A child did not belong to one set of parents, but to all of the family. Since all the adults in the family were considered parents of all the children, there was no trauma in sharing. Both the family and the greater community took part in raising and educating the children. If a child showed interest or talent in a particular direction, the child was encouraged to follow it. This meant that a child was often cared for by someone other than the biological parents. For instance, if a child was always playing with plants, she might go to live with an "auntie," who was an herbalist. Or if a child was more interested in building things, he might be placed with an "uncle" to learn how to build canoes. If a child showed an interest in the spiritual realm, she might go to live with a *kahuna* and be trained as a priest. The child's interest and abilities were always considered in the placement.

> **Life centered around the family.**

Because they lived on islands, the Hawaiian families resided close to one another. Life centered around the family. In *Tales of the Night Rainbow*, Pali Jae Lee and Koko Willis have set down the oral traditions of the *'Ohana Kame'ekua* (*Kame'ekua* Family) on the Island of Moloka'i. These were stories that were passed down to the family by their "Big Granma," *Kaili'ohe Kame'ekua*. She was chosen at a young age to learn the genealogical and historical chants of her family. We are grateful to *Kaili'ohe* and her descendants for preserving this important history of Hawaiian values and family life.

According to *Kaili'ohe*, on the Island of Moloka'i, families were the social, political and spiritual units of life. Children were taught to take pride in their families and their clan. Several generations often lived together in the same household. These households made up the greater family unit. The *Kapuna* Elders ruled the family. These were people who had distinguished themselves by years of "hard work and wise thinking." They were known for being "loving and unselfish in all things." They had mastered the secrets and history of the family. These *Kapuna* were the leaders of the family and their decisions were never questioned. They were believed to posses the greatest knowledge and the greatest *mana*. The ruling Elders handled all disputes within the family and all disputes with outsiders.

The Elders also made important family decisions, such as choosing the sacred name of each child. This sacred name was not revealed to the child until he or she was ready to hear it. The Elders watched the children, seeing what they did well and what interested them. They used this information to place a child with an uncle or auntie, who could teach them about a particular knowledge, a craft, or a spiritual path. The Elders also insured that each member of the family remembered the family teachings and history.

This is one of the family teachings:

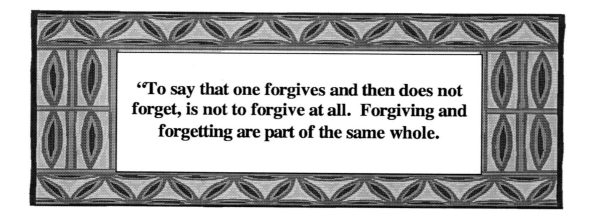

"To say that one forgives and then does not forget, is not to forgive at all. Forgiving and forgetting are part of the same whole.

The Elders held the "heart of the family," both the living family and the spirit family. Family members who had passed into spirit were considered an important part of the family. They were remembered before food was eaten and in *mele* and chants. They were spoken of often and asked for advice and help by the living family members.

When a family meeting was called, everyone attended. Once a year there was a large gathering of the families in the *Makahiki* season, a time when no wars were permitted. This was a time of great celebration, of rejoicing, merriment, remembering and romancing. Young people fell in love and many were married. There were sports contests, feasts and fun. New members were introduced and the ones who had passed into spirit were remembered. Each family line was presented to the group and its genealogy recited. The old chants were sung telling of the family history and heritage.

The family was an integral part of each person's life. Members of the family helped one another "be at peace within," especially when a person was ready to pass into spirit. Within the family all natural sisters and brothers, half-sisters and half-brothers, and first cousins were all

> **There is one body of life to which we all belong.**

called "sisters and brothers." All the members of the generation of the parents were called *"Makua"* or parents. All the members of the generation of the grandparents were called *"Kapuna"* or grandparents. A child loved all the members of his family and they all loved the child. He understood by this love that "there was one body of life to which we all belong."

The family was a communal society. Most of the family possessions were owned together. When a child was born, he was given a woven mat for sleeping on, a *kapa* blanket, and a calabash for eating. These belonged to the child and were regarded as an extension of his person. No one touched another's personal possessions without permission. No one would step on another's mat or touch his *kapa*. When a person traveled away from home, he always took his personal possessions with him.

If a person stole the belongings of another, he was banished forever from the family by the Elders. Stealing personal possessions was the highest crime. The banished person was shunned by the rest of the family and virtually became invisible. It would be as if he or she never existed. People punished in this manner often committed suicide or simply vanished forever. It was a terrible crime and a terrible punishment.

When a man and woman wanted to marry, they simply agreed to share a sleeping mat beneath the same *kapa* and they were considered married. It was a great decision to allow someone else to share your mat and *kapa*. A woman was never forced to do anything against her will. If she wanted a divorce, she stopped sleeping under the same *kapa* as her husband. She moved into a different household and married someone else.

There were no single-parent homes, orphans or widows in the Hawaiian society. If a man died, his widow and all her children were taken in by either a brother, son or cousin. She was considered then to be the "wife" of the man of that household with all status, rights and privileges. All adult women who lived in a man's household were considered his "wives," no matter their ages. When a man wanted to take a wife, but that left sister or mother alone, these women were also taken into the new household. A woman always had the right to refuse to "bed with a man" or to leave if she chose another.

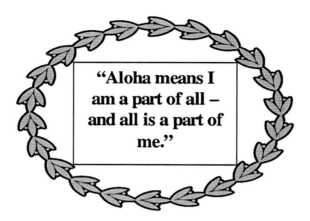

"Aloha means I am a part of all – and all is a part of me."

All the family members were teachers of the children. Life was their school and they learned everything from the *'Ohana*. Children were taught by example and with stories and parables. As soon as a child began to speak, he was taught about "*aloha*." *Aloha* means that "I am a part of all – and all is a part of me." They were taught about the love of family, love of the land and sea, and to love and respect themselves and everything around them. They were taught not to ask another to do for them what they could do for themselves. They were also taught that there is no dividing line between two people.

This is another family teaching:

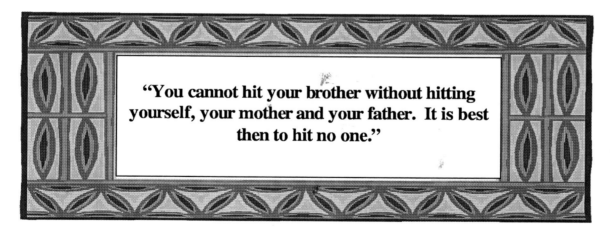

"You cannot hit your brother without hitting yourself, your mother and your father. It is best then to hit no one."

The rules of the family were easy to learn. Everyone was free to come and go as they pleased as long as they did no harm to another. Children learned that "people, their feelings, the family, and the soul's growth" were the most important things. A person cannot be involved with things (possessions) and retain control of his or her heart and mind. They learned to act with respect toward the world around them. Everything that grew on the land or swam in the sea was called sister and brother. They learned not to destroy or waste anything. If a plant were needed, they were taught the proper way to talk to it, to explain why it was being picked, and to thank it for its gift. They were taught to talk to the animals and fish and even the beings of the mineral world in the same manner.

Children were also taught about personal power. If a child's personal power (*mana*) was strong and they believed in themselves as powerful beings, they could accomplish anything. Children, who were taught these ways, could call the sea turtle and the shark, manipulate the clouds and winds to bring rain, move heavy objects with ease, and make objects disappear and reappear again. They often spent hours in contests against each other practicing these skills. When they wished to change their circumstances, they were taught to release their present conditions.

> **To change circumstances, you have to replace current conditions.**

As soon as a child began to talk, his dreams were discussed with him. Dreams were considered important teachers. Learning took place in dreams. A person is shown his errors and how to correct them through dreams. Some dreams gave clues as to what the child would become as an adult. The names of all children came through dreams. Help or warnings came in dreams. It was believed that signs and omens appeared in dreams that effected the entire family.

As a child grew and was placed with an adult to gain more knowledge, she was given rules in order to learn self-discipline. Without self-discipline a person was considered incomplete. The following rules were taught to *Kaili'ohe* and other children in training.

1. Learn to do what you are told the first time.
2. Learn to listen and not talk back.
3. Learn patience, cooperation, understanding and service.
4. Do your task without grumbling.
5. Do not argue with your Elders.
6. Learn to understand other people, be in tune with them and the environment.
7. Always show kindness and concern.

These traditional child rearing practices and teachings are just as important to us in the Western world. Pride in family and heritage; responsibility to ourselves and to others; sharing what we have; respecting our Elders; respecting the personal possessions of others; honoring the environment in which we live; staying connected to the world of Spirit; and, understanding personal power are all important concepts to teach our Inner Selves and our offspring. Other concepts, such as looking for the special talents and abilities of our Selves to show us the best way to nurture and develop them, are also invaluable lessons to learn from traditional Hawaiian families.

The knowledge of *Huna* and the values of traditional Hawaiian families are two of the greatest nurturing tools we can possess. *Huna* provides an efficient and positive method for self nurturing and personal growth. The knowledge of the Three Selves teaches us how to develop a proper and loving inner relationship. *Huna* helps us understand the psychological actions of others. It provides a solid spiritual base for living. It is an ethical and moral guideline that embraces the principles of responsible thought and action, loving service, and the power of forgiveness. Hawaiian family values offer us guidelines for living in community with other Selves. These values show us the way to truly live the loving, "no hurt," and helpful life, which is so important in nurturing our Inner Family.

---

**The *Huna* Way is to live the loving ,"no hurt," and helpful life.**

---

# THE MOTHERING PRINCIPLE AND THE *'UNIHIPILI*

"Mother is the name for God in the lips and hearts of children."
-W.M. Thackery

The spiritual definition of Mother is "a symbol of the feminine or receptive aspect of the manifesting Spirit of the One. The Mothering Principle directs human evolution. She shines forth and is the means of awakening the faint beginnings of true life in the soul. She is the brooding, nourishing element of Divine Mind, or God, in which spiritual ideals are brought to fruition. She is the Goddess Principle." (*Dictionary of All Scriptures and Myths* and *The Revealing Word.*)

In *Huna*, the mother is all of these definitions and more. The Mothering Principle is the ever-present, all-loving aspect of the Higher Self, the *'Aumakua*. The *'Aumakua* is an integrated wholeness of the higher qualities, divine characteristics, and *mana-loa* of both female and male, mother and father. The Mothering aspect of the *'Aumakua* is our Holy Mother. She is the "very embodiment of perfect love." One ancient religious text says that the Spirit of God is "like a mother's breath on her newborn."

The Mothering Principle of our *'Aumakua* is always there for us, she never fails. She nurtures, supports, and loves us for who we are. She provides guidance to us in the areas of higher emotions, intimacy, and cooperative relationships. She receives and cares for our prayers nourishing them with *mana-loa* until the Fathering Principle encourages, directs, and presses down the answers into the physical world of our future. We learn the higher aspects of nurturing from the Mothering Principle.

21

It is from the Mothering Principle that we learn about the emotional Self, the *'Unihipili*. The Mothering Principle teaches of the inner world, of emotions, of the sensory and extrasensory, of love, trust, and service. We learn how to respond internally to Spirit from the heart perspective of the mother.

> **It is from the mother we learn about the *'Unihipili*.**

Before a woman can become a true representative of the Mothering Principle, she must first become an integrated human being. A woman's first responsibility is to care for her Inner Selves. It is her responsibility to love and understand her *'Unihipili*. It is her responsibility to love and understand her *'Uhane* and learn to use her logic in harmony with her emotions. It is her responsibility to maintain the connection with her *'Aumakua* and bring the spiritual into her life.

A woman's second responsibility is to discover and follow her Purpose. Following her Purpose leads to acquiring the education she needs to insure an independent financial life for herself and any children she may bring into the world. Women can no longer depend on men to support them and their children. A woman is responsible to share her Purpose with the world despite her role as a mother.

The third responsibility of a woman is to nurture her primary relationship. It is through this relationship that she fully realizes her feminine nature and learns to understand and honor the masculine. It is from the harmony of male/female energy that we learn the basics of the next step in evolution, that of becoming an *'Aumakua*. In order for each of us to graduate or evolve to the next level of consciousness, we must understand, respect and appreciate the Mothering Principle of the *'Aumakua*. We do this by observing, understanding, and experiencing the role of the mother on the physical plane.

> **Mother is the first nurturer of life.**

The mother is the first nurturer of life. The biology of the human female and her specific characteristics enable her body to be the vehicle through which the new spirit enters the world. The child grows in the womb of his mother and is nurtured by her very life. We learn how to nurture our Inner Selves by understanding the nurturing perspective of the mother.

The role of the mother is critical to the development of the Inner Selves. They are totally dependent on their mother during the period of gestation. Recent scientific opinion suggests that an infant is not fully developed at the time of birth. It suggests that the full development of the baby is completed nine months **after** birth. The baby is born at the end of the first nine months, not because he is fully developed, but because the size of the brain and the body is limited inside the womb. If the baby continued to grow, it would be physically impossible for a mother to give birth. It is imperative that a child continues to be nurtured by his mother for the second nine months. The Inner Selves remain dependent on the mother until about age three when the *'Uhane* is strong enough to take its rightful place. The *'Unihipili* then changes its dependency from the mother's *'Uhane* to its own *'Uhane*. The lessons the *'Unihipili* learns from the mother will be the basis for all subsequent learning, including its outlook on life.

The gender characteristics of a woman make her naturally suited to the role of mother. Tine Thevenin in her book, *Mothering and Fathering*, states that both men and women have a unique and different perspective on life. She suggests the following gender characteristics that shape and define a woman and make her suited to be a mother.

# GENDER CHARACTERISTICS OF WOMEN

1.  Women desire nurturing, bonding and closeness.
2.  They seek intimacy and connectedness.
3.  They measure success by the strength of their connectedness.
4.  Women are naturally empathetic.
5.  Women believe the purpose of communication is to establish and maintain connection, intimacy and rapport.
6.  They are other-focused.
7.  They talk to support one another.
8.  Women give information to help others.
9.  They want support.
10. They strive for interaction.
11. Women want to be liked and admired.
12. They want to receive approval for their efforts.
13. They believe that freedom means less worry.
14. Women have the ability for simultaneous multiple involvements
15. They have a capacity for higher stress levels.
16. Their senses are more acute than a man's, including the extra senses.
17. Women are more aware of subtle changes even when they are asleep.
18. They pick up more quickly on subtle messages of moods, emotions, and the needs of others.
19. Women place greater value on interdependence.

Women are shaped by their focus on relationships with others. They place greater value on interdependence, nurturing, and communication for connection. They are more in touch with their emotions and can access them easily. They are highly sensitive to energies. They have a deep connection with nature. These are all qualities of the *'Unihipili*. To fully understand and honor our *'Unihipili*, we must understand and honor the female characteristics and qualities.

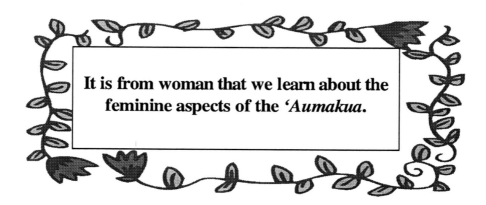

It is from woman that we learn about the feminine aspects of the *'Aumakua*.

Women need to understand and honor their own female characteristics. They also need to understand and honor the qualities of the *'Uhane* and the characteristics of men. By doing so they will be able to uplift thought and logic and integrate the qualities of the *'Unihipili* with the *'Uhane*. Men must understand and honor the qualities of the *'Unihipili* and the characteristics of women to gain strength from their emotions and integrate heart and mind.

The ability of a woman to nurture forms the strong mother/infant bond that is so important to the development of a human being. Selma Fraiberg, child development specialist, says, "When early bonding with Mother occurs and is free of frustration, anger, disappointment and fear of abandonment, a child stands a much better chance of finding secure love as an adult." It has only been in recent years that scientists have "discovered" the importance of a strong mother/infant bond. All subsequent learning and intellectual development depends on this bond. A baby's outlook on the world depends on this bond. All future relationships depend on this bond. Children need their mothers. Daughters especially need their mothers to help them grow into womanhood.

> **All subsequent learning depends on the mother/infant bond.**

The basic foundation of the child's personality is being formed in his earliest interchanges with his nurturing mother. In *Huna*, we understand this to mean the personality of the *'Unihipili*. This shaping of personality occurs as the mother responds to the child's needs. If she responds promptly and gently, he learns he is important and cherished. He learns the world is a happy and caring place.

Being a nurturer also means knowing when to let go. Mothers have an instinctive ability to gauge when a child is ready to let go and move out on his own. Whether it is in weaning, learning to walk, going off to school, marrying, or passing on, a mother knows she must release her child to his own life. She is able to release because she knows the *'Aumakua* of the child will continue to guard, guide, and protect him.

A woman's nurturing energy creates bonding, closeness, and interconnectedness. A woman is naturally other-focused and possesses an inherent ability to be intimate. All of these gifts a child needs to receive from a woman. All of these gifts we need to give our Inner Selves. It is only through bonding, closeness, and interconnectedness that we form a true communication system between the Selves. The *'Unihipili* learns from his mother that love is unlimited and it is through love that we stay connected. We take this knowledge with us when we evolve to the level of the *'Aumakua*. The Mothering Principle of the *'Aumakua* expresses love on a grander scale. It is through interconnectedness that we realize the Oneness of all life.

A *Huna* mother knows, that in addition to learning physical skills and social behavior, a child needs to learn how to listen and talk to his Three Selves. He needs these inner skills in order to become a complete person. It is the ability to communicate internally that makes us effective human beings. The mother is the first teacher of *Huna* communication skills. The earlier this internal communication begins, the better.

The ability to deal with and communicate with our emotional Self, our *'Unihipili*, is called "emotional intelligence" by Daniel Goleman, who claims that emotional intelligence is more important than intellectual intelligence for a child's development. Goleman defines emotional intelligence as "being able to rein in emotional impulses...to be able to read another's innermost feelings...and, to handle relationships smoothly." He

> **Emotional Intelligence is important to our development.**

says that the emotional lessons we learn as children at home and in school shape our emotional circuits, which are at the center of all intelligence.

Nurturing is about supporting the development of both the *'Uhane* and *'Unihipili*. It is about understanding feelings and teaching relationship. "The emotional ability to depend on others is an enrichment of life," explains Elaine Heffner, author of *Mothering: The Emotional Experience of Motherhood After Freud and Feminism*. She says that total dependency exists only in infancy and total independence never exists. Our mother teaches us early lessons about trust, love, and service. These lessons are not taught by her words, but by her actions. The *'Unihipili* and *'Uhane* learn these early lessons through the symbolic actions of their mother.

Mothers are lavishly loving and gently firm. They focus on interconnectedness and emotional experience. They are intuitive and rely on their instincts. They are models of the *'Unihipili* and representative of the qualities of the Mothering Principle of the *'Aumakua* on earth. To become good nurturers we must understand the Mothering Principle and how this Principle relates to the characteristics of the *'Unihipili*. We must learn how to apply the female perspective to nurture our Inner Selves.

# THE FATHERING PRINCIPLE AND THE *'UHANE*

"It is a wise father that knows his own child."
--William Shakespeare

The spiritual definition of Father is "a symbol of the masculine, or directing aspect of the manifesting Spirit, which nurtures thought and the true idea about Being. The father is the bridge between the inner and outer worlds. It is the father or masculine energy that fights injustice in the world and creates a haven for Truth and Love. The father is the Directing Principle of God." (*Dictionary of All Scriptures and Myths*)

In *Huna* the Fathering Principle is the all-loving and ever-present male aspect of the *'Aumakua*, the High Self. The Father aspect of our *'Aumakua* is our Holy Father, who is always encouraging, inspiring, and directing us. He nurtures, comforts and protects us. He provides guidance to us in the areas of higher thoughts, purpose, and expansion. He gathers our prayers, infuses them with life-giving *mana-loa* and presses down or directs the answers into our future using his Holy Will.

It is from the Fathering Principle that we learn about the rational and logical Self – the *'Uhane*. The Fathering Principle introduces us to the outer world, teaches us how the mind functions to solve problems, how to use deductive reasoning, how to speak and use the power of words, and how to shape and use our Will. The Fathering Principle teaches us about personal power and how to use it for good. We learn to respond to Spirit from the mind perspective of the Fathering Principle, as we learn to respond to Spirit from the heart perspective of the Mothering Principle.

We need to understand, respect and appreciate the Fathering Principle of the *'Aumakua* in order to graduate or evolve to the next level of consciousness. We do this by observing and

| The father is the bridge to the outer world. |
| :---: |

understanding the role of the father on the physical plane. The father is the bridge to the outer world. He represents the adventure of the great unknown, the eternal curiosity about things outside oneself, the power of determination and persistence. The father is protector, comforter and provider. He is our second teacher who leads us to the outside world and shows us how to reach for the stars.

Every child needs his father and all that his father can provide. A child cannot learn all he needs to know about the world without his father. He cannot take the next step towards independence and autonomy without the nurturing guidance of his father. A son especially needs his father to help him grow into manhood.

Tine Thevenin describes the gender characteristics of males. These characteristics make them ideal fathers. They are very different from the gender characteristics of females.

 **GENDER CHARACTERISTICS OF MEN**

1. Men emphasize independence.
2. Men encourage expansion and achievement through competition.
3. They seek challenges.
4. They strive for higher accomplishments.
5. Men are concerned with status, how they fit into the scheme of things.
6. They rely on their own minds and resources to solve problems.
7. They respect intelligence and logic.
8. They aim for health and vigor.
9. Men strive for order and the direction that comes from order.
10. They tend to be self-focused, rather than other-focused.
11. Men appreciate rules and regulations.
12. They communicate to give information in order to solve problems.
13. They negotiate for status in a hierarchical order.
14. Men believe freedom means less dependency.

15. Men instruct, rather than suggest.
16. They stress control.
17. They want to earn respect.

Men strive for information in order to solve problems. They approach situations wanting to know where they stand in relationship to others. Men instruct, stress control, are inventive, prefer rules and regulations, and are good negotiators. They rely on their own minds and resources to solve problems. All of these qualities are qualities of the *'Uhane*. To more fully understand and honor our *'Uhane*, we must understand and honor the male characteristics.

A man's gender characteristics emphasize expansion, challenge, achievement, the search for higher positions, and independence. He is other-focused or outwardly focused. He is self-reliant, self-sufficient, intelligent and logical. All of these characteristics qualify men to be fathers.

Men see independence as exciting, posing challenges, and offering rewards. Independence gives a person feelings of self-mastery. Independence fosters exploration and curiosity. Independence is a great and noble aspiration for a human being. It is part of our birthright. It is proper for a father to teach independence. It is proper for us to teach our Inner Selves independence. However, independence comes only when our *'Uhane* has matured sufficiently to understand it.

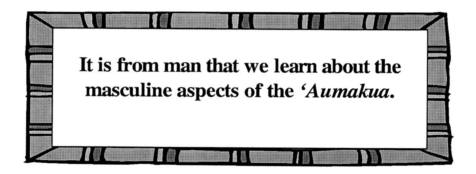

**It is from man that we learn about the masculine aspects of the *'Aumakua*.**

Thevenin says, "As a child grows and expands his world away from his mother, he needs another human being who is equally trustworthy and encourages the development of independence, making him ready for the transition to adulthood. In the security of his father's love a child receives the encouragement, support, and trust he needs to venture out and grow up." Every child needs the influence and love of his father. He needs the special kind of male energy only a father can share. It is the father energy that expands and challenges a child. He teaches the child how to be self-reliant, responsible and logical. Fathers have the answers to the big WHY questions.

We need the masculine energy of the *'Uhane* to expand and challenge us. We need to learn how to deal with the world on a logical, rational basis so that we can anticipate the consequences of our words, thoughts and actions before we engage them. We learn to reach for higher thoughts and ideals through the male qualities of the *'Uhane*. The fundamental value of the father is his ability to maintain the "connection to elsewhere." He is the means by which the inner power is made manifest in the outer world. The father energy paves the way for the *daimon* of the Selves to express Purpose.

> **We need the masculine energy to express our Purpose.**

Before a man can become a true representative of the Fathering Principle, he must first become an integrated human being with a healthy physical body and a high energy level. It is a man's first responsibility to care for his Inner Selves. It is his responsibility to love and understand his *'Unihipili* and gain strength from his emotional Self, in order to become whole. It is his responsibility to uplift his *'Uhane* to higher levels of thought, word and deed. It is his responsibility to maintain a strong connection to his *'Aumakua* and bring the spiritual into his life. It is often difficult for a man to be strong in his Spiritual life, but he must become a model for masculine spirituality for his Inner Selves and his children.

Pursuing and expressing his own Purpose is a man's second responsibility. So many men have become addicted to spectator sports and activities that their Purpose languishes and is sometimes forgotten. Other men immerse themselves in careers or jobs and have neglected to discover and fulfill their Purpose. Without Purpose a man's life is empty. If a man can combine Purpose with career, he is indeed fortunate.

> **A man must learn to share his energy in appropriate ways.**

A man next nurtures the relationship with his wife or partner, being aware of the subtleties of a woman's emotions and her special needs. It is in listening and becoming aware, without taking action, that he learns about the feminine perspective. He must learn to share his masculine energy with his partner and not just take her feminine energy. Commitment to his primary relationship prepares a man for his next step in evolution – to become an *'Aumakua*.

In order to evolve to the next level of consciousness, we all must understand, respect and appreciate the Fathering Principle. We do this by observing and understanding the role of the father as a parent on the physical plane. After taking care of his body, following his Purpose, and nurturing the relationship with his partner, a man is ready to nurture his Inner Selves and his children. In today's society, men are often fulfilling the roles of mother, father, step-father, or foster-father. Many fathers are also absent from their families. The absence of good father role models is adversely affecting our society. Boys are growing up without their fathers. They grow up physically but do not grow up emotionally or logically. They do not have their fathers to teach them how to be a man. The father models the male attitudes, language and actions for his son. He models the qualities of the *'Uhane* and the higher

> **We need our Fathers!**

aspects of the *'Aumakua*. Without this model boys cannot grow up properly and learn how to nurture and integrate their Inner Selves.

The Inner Selves learn all the developmental skills they need to know when they have <u>both</u> their mother and father. Fathers have a special role to play for the Inner Family and for their earthly family. Fathers show children through word and deed what a "committed family relationship" is all about. Fathers model commitment, while mothers model persistence. Masculine and feminine energies interact with each other to create a harmonious and strong support system for the Selves.

To nurture means to "foster growth." Nurturing the Inner Selves means to support and love them. It means to teach them as they mature from infancy to adulthood. Fathers teach about the *'Uhane* by exemplifying the qualities of that Self. How a male *'Uhane* relates to the *'Unihipili*, to the *'Aumakua*, to his partner, his children, and his community are learned from the life of the father. Fathers teach *'Uhane* skills for handling anger and aggression and other volatile emotions of the *'Unihipili*. They encourage appropriate challenges and acknowledge the efforts of the *'Unihipili*. They take an active interest in the ongoing feelings of the *'Unihipili*. They demonstrate cooperation through love in action. A father teaches how to maintain the connection to Spirit through his own spiritual life. He teaches us how to structure the pattern of a prayer and the steps to create an effective prayer. He teaches us the importance of forgiveness in the prayer process. He is the earthly model for the Fathering principle of the *'Aumakua*.

# COMMUNICATING WITH THE SELVES

"Successful communication doesn't necessarily mean talking."

Communication is critical to the proper development of the Inner Selves. The *'Uhane* communicates with words and talks to the *'Unihipili*, who does understand their meanings. The *'Unihipili* cannot use words because it cannot speak. All communication from the *'Unihipili* is in the form of symbols and feelings. Feelings can be strong and full of energy, or subtle and soft in the form of gentle nudges. Symbols appear in dreams. The *'Unihipili* can direct the attention of the *'Uhane* to a symbol in the outer world as a means of conveying its message. When you speak out loud as the *'Uhane* to your *'Unihipili*, it knows something important is happening. We should all be talking out loud to our *'Unihipili* every day. The *'Uhane* and *'Unihipili* also communicate with each other in the center of the limbic brain where the two hemispheres intersect. This is where we engage in that silent inner dialogue. We also communicate with the Inner Selves of others through words, symbols, and feelings.

Mothers and fathers can communicate with the Inner Selves of their children while they are still in the womb. Current scientific opinion states that a fetus in the womb has no intelligence, therefore it cannot be influenced by outside factors. The theory goes on to say that after birth a baby is a "clean slate" waiting to be written upon by environmental, social, and psychological factors. We know through the study of *Huna*, that an unborn baby possesses two intelligent minds. You <u>can</u> communicate with an unborn baby through feelings, images, sounds (not words), and movements. The unborn baby may communicate with you through dreams or feelings. The unborn *'Unihipili* is sensitive to feelings, especially those charged with negative or positive energy. When you are sending feelings to an unborn child, they should be calm, serene, happy and loving. The *'Uhane* of the unborn child is not fully in the body at that time and cannot help the *'Unihipili* differentiate between its own feelings and the feelings it is receiving from the outside.

We communicate with older *'Unihipili* in the same ways. Children receive strong feeling communications from other *'Unihipili.* They become cranky if the feelings of the adults around them are agitated. They will burst into tears if they are in a group of people who are feeling sad. They will also become hyperactive in a group of people who are feeling happy and joyful. Feeling communications are stored as memories along with other sensory input.

As adults our *'Unihipili* reacts to feeling communications from others. We have shut out these communications so long that the *'Unihipili* often doesn't bother to bring the messages to our attention. If we listen with our inner ears we can sense these feeling messages coming to us. This is part of the extrasensory ability of our *'Unihipili.* Feeling messages must be interpreted by our *'Uhane* in order for us to understand their content. Often the interpretation is not correct depending on how well our *'Uhane* has learned to listen. Because our *'Unihipili* is our psychic Self, it also uses symbols to communicate. Much of this symbolic communication occurs in dreams. All the symbols, colors and feelings in your dreams are messages from your *'Unihipili.*

**Singing, images, music, energy and movement are all forms of nonverbal communication.**

Sounds are another form of nonverbal communication. Animals use sounds to communicate as do birds and other creatures, often out of the range of human ears. Humans also use sounds for basic communication. We grunt our disapproval or click our tongue in sympathy. Music is a form of communication. The sound of your words and the tone and melody of the music communicate feelings and moods. Music has a beneficial effect on both the emotional and intellectual brains. Classical music has been proven to raise the IQ of the *'Uhane* and to soothe the troubled emotions of the *'Unihipili.* If you play a musical instrument, your *'Unihipili* will enjoy listening to the mood of your music and may even nudge you to select a particular piece of music to express its mood. Primitive instruments, such as drums, offer the Selves a form of basic communication. Primitive music draws us into an altered state where we can communicate on a different level. Music is a good way to daily communicate with your Inner Selves.

Every culture in the world enjoys singing. Singing is an important part of communicating about life. Everyone sings, whether in the shower, driving to work, or around the campfire. Our *'Unihipili* loves to sing because singing combines sound and energy. Families who sing together benefit from the closeness of the activity and from sharing the energy created by the song, the power-filled words, and the melody. Songs effect us in many ways. Lullabies soothe and comfort; comic songs make us laugh; romantic ballads remind us of love; patriotic songs stir deep emotions; band marches arouse us; and, songs of Spirit inspire us. Singing is one form of communication in which both the *'Unihipili* and *'Uhane* can participate together. Singing lifts our hearts and minds in higher communication to the spiritual world of the 'Aumakua.

Energy or *mana* is a form of communication. *Mana* flows in and through all life and can be generated by and directed by the Selves. Positive or negative *mana* can be sent to our Inner Selves and to the Inner Selves of other people. The 'Unihipili naturally shares *mana* with the 'Uhane and 'Aumakua. This sharing of *mana* with the other Selves is a message of love. Parents naturally share *mana* with their children. Spouses share *mana* with each other. Sometimes we receive or send *mana* messages that contain emotions. These messages are very clear to the 'Unihipili who receives them. These are usually messages for help. If our 'Uhane is able to discern these messages, our Inner Selves can work together to help whoever sent them. These messages of feeling and energy should never go answered.

Movement is another form of communication. The best actors know how to combine movement, emotion and words to illustrate a character's reactions. Mimes are excellent examples of how to communicate through movement. Babies receive messages of comfort when they are rocked. Men and women give clear messages of love or enjoyment when they dance together. Athletic games are movement messages. Everyone understands movement messages, no matter what language they speak. Movement speaks to us on a cellular level. We are governed by movement messages from the tides, the cycles of night and day, and the cycle of birth and death.

**Prayer is a powerful tool for communication.**

Prayer is a powerful tool for communication. Prayer effects us on a molecular and spiritual level. Scientific research has proven conclusively that prayer works! The best prayers, according to the research, are more general in content, asking for the highest good to be done. We know through the study of *Huna* that the 'Aumakua, in its infinite wisdom, sees the larger picture for us and can draw on sources we cannot even comprehend to bring about our highest good. Therefore, we allow the 'Aumakua to use its higher abilities to bring this good into our lives. Daily prayers of thanksgiving should be sent regularly to our 'Aumakua. Gratitude is one of the highest forms of communication to our Inner Selves and to our 'Aumakua.

Daily meditation and prayer are spiritual communications with our Higher Self. These forms of communication are critical to the development of the Inner Selves. They also help us stay in daily contact with our Divine Parent, who is ready to guide, nurture, love, and direct us whenever we ask. Meditation and prayer keep us in touch with our spiritual nature. We know that every thought and word is a prayer of communication to our Higher Self. We must remind our Inner Selves that this kind of communication is very powerful and that we want positive energy to go out from our hearts and minds in messages of love for all humankind.

# PHASES OF HUMAN DEVELOPMENT

"To everything there is a season, and a time for every purpose under heaven."
– The Bible

The term "phases of human development" refers to the physical, emotional, intellectual, and social skill periods a human grows through from conception to elderhood. As nurturers of our Inner Selves, it is important to understand these phases of development and how the skills of one phase build on the previous skills. It is exciting to observe the *'Unihipili* and *'Uhane* as they learn to manipulate the physical body and to develop a system of cooperation between the intellectual and emotional minds.

The Selves learn through interaction. Each interaction between *'Unihipili* and *'Uhane*, and between the Selves and the environment, is a critical interaction no matter how small. The *'Unihipili* stores the interaction as memory and the *'Uhane* interprets the impressions based on this memory. Each event teaches something to the developing Selves. By mastering the simple skills of each phase of development, the Selves move on to more complex intellectual and emotional learning. Most adults don't realize that even newborn Selves are accomplishing remarkable feats of learning. Childhood learning appears to be simple "playing." To the Inner Selves of the child however, these "playing" activities are experimental and concentrated modalities of intense learning patterns. We can best help the Inner Selves by providing educational opportunities appropriate to that phase of development. If our Inner Selves have not learned the skills of a particular phase, we can return to that age and remaster those skills.

The physical development of a person depends on the ability to master certain motor skills. This process is, in reality, the ability of the *'Unihipili* and *'Uhane* to work with and to control the physical body. It begins in the womb and progresses throughout life. We see these motor skills rapidly developing in infancy. The physical skills are learned by the Selves without any outside assistance.

Since we have two minds or consciousnesses residing in the body, we have the responsibility as nurturers to provide learning opportunities for both minds. Most educational systems in the past have been geared toward the intellectual mind, but in recent years the importance of emotional education has been widely accepted. Daniel Goleman reports on emotional intelligence or EQ in his book, *Emotional Intelligence*. Goleman says, "In a sense we have two brains, two minds – and two different kinds of intelligence: rational and emotional. How we do in life is determined by both – it is not just IQ but emotional intelligence (EQ) that matters. Indeed, intellect cannot work at its best without emotional intelligence."

Goleman also points out that our "passions, when well exercised, have wisdom, they guide our thinking, our values, our survival…the emotional and rational operate in tight harmony, intertwining their different ways of knowing to guide us through the world." The *kahuna* would agree with him. This is a good description of the *Huna* concept of how the *'Unihipili* and *'Uhane* work together. We know that emotion is crucial to effective thought, both in making wise decisions and in simply allowing us to think clearly. The rational mind evolved out of the emotional mind. The "biological pathways that make the mind, the emotions, and the body are not separate, but are intimately intertwined." The central nervous system and the immune system are part of this greater system and are affected by all the other systems.

> **Emotion is crucial to effective thought.**

The **intellectual lessons** we learn as children at home and in school shape the intellectual circuits in the body. But the *'Uhane* has more to learn than just logic. The *'Uhane* must also learn to direct, control and exercise its Will. It must learn to uplift and expand its thoughts and ideas. We must provide our *'Uhane* with opportunities to learn these lessons as well.

> **We grow by learning lessons of mind and heart.**

The **emotional lessons** we learn as children at home and in school shape the emotional circuits in the body. These emotional circuits are "sculpted by experience" throughout our lives, especially during our childhood. The most basic lessons of emotional life are laid down in the intimate moments – the small, repeated exchanges that take place between parent and child. Most critical are those that let the *'Unihipili* know its emotions are met with empathy and acceptance and are reciprocated through attunement with the mother. We don't dare leave these experiences to chance. We must provide our *'Unihipili* with positive experiences.

We understand that the wisdom of the 'Aumakua is unalterably intertwined with the other two minds. The realization of the spiritual in our lives is a great step toward wholeness. We must integrate all Three Selves in order to become whole. It is imperative that we teach our Inner Selves how to bring the 'Aumakua into its rightful place and live our life guided by higher Mind.

The 'Uhane and 'Unihipili combine intellectual and emotional intelligence and their separate talents and abilities right from the beginning. They must work together to be able to manage the complexities of the human body to exist in this world. It is important to look at the phases of development in relation to the development of the combined 'Uhane – 'Unihipili. We see how the 'Uhane develops its abilities of logic and discernment and claims its rightful place as guide and teacher. We observe the patience and persistence of the 'Unihipili as it refines the body and claims its rightful place as information specialist and emotion controller. We see how the 'Aumakua is an integral and vital part of each human life as it takes its rightful place as Divine Parent and guardian of the future.

**We see how the Three Selves combine and integrate mind and heart and spirit to become whole.**

The following phases of human development come from the book by psychologists Barbara and Philip Newman, *Phases of Development: A Psychosocial Approach.* I refer to them because they give a good breakdown of developmental ages. I have renamed some of the phases. The age ranges are guidelines for understanding the skill building process. Each of us in unique and develops at a different rate. Each of us follows our own Purpose and acquires just the right level of skills, talents, and abilities for our own life. Our 'Uhane and 'Unihipili work together, guided by our 'Aumakua, through the phases using the physical body to further refine the development of the two minds.

```
┌─────────────────────────────────────────────────┐
│            PHASES OF HUMAN DEVELOPMENT            │
│                                                   │
│  Prenatal ...............................0 to birth        │
│  Infancy.............................birth to 2 years      │
│  Toddlerhood ............................. 3-5      years  │
│  Primary School Age ................ 6-8      years        │
│  Middle School Age .................9-12      years        │
│  Teen Age Adolescence......... 12-17      years           │
│  Mature Adolescence ............ 17-22      years          │
│  Early Adulthood................... 22-30      years       │
│  Mature Adulthood................ 30-50      years         │
│  Elderhood .............................50 +      years    │
│                                                   │
└─────────────────────────────────────────────────┘
```

In the following sections we discuss the different ages of human development and the characteristics of that phase. We explore how the *'Uhane* and *'Unihipili* develop in each phase and see which skills they need to master before going on to the next. We offer suggestions on how to facilitate the process of mastery. At the end of each section are techniques for returning to that phase and remastering the skills.

Self-esteem is a quality of the *'Unihipili* and you need to listen carefully to what your *'Unihipili* tells you about its self-esteem. One of the ways we can tell if we have not mastered a development skill is by evaluating the quality of our self-esteem. Psychologist Stanley Coopersmith explains that self-esteem is based on the following factors:

1. Maternal certainty about child rearing practices.
2. Minimal daily conflicts within the family.
3. Close relationships with siblings.
4. Close relationships with peers.
5. Expression of parental acceptance and warmth.
6. Firm and consistent discipline, which sets clear limits for behavior.
7. Involvement of the child in family decisions.

To this list I would add:

8. Respect for the child as an expression of God or Spirit.
9. Respect for both the emotional and intellectual minds of the child.
10. Understanding that the two Selves are already fully intelligent at conception.

We will return to this list later.

If either of the Inner Selves has not mastered the skills of any phase of development, we may get stuck in that phase. We are unbalanced and cannot move forward. This causes problems if we have already reached adulthood. Both Selves must master the appropriate skills and progress through the phases or we cannot become whole. We can use the knowledge of *Huna* to bring balance back into our lives. This process is part of nurturing. Nurturing means to lovingly support the growth of our Inner Selves and help them master the skills they need.

The process of remastery is simple, but takes time, persistence, and energy. It takes commitment to your own personal growth. First, you gain the cooperation of your emotional Self, your *'Unihipili.* You do this by simply asking and then listening for the answer. If you are not accustomed to listening to your *'Unihipili,* you can use other methods to insure you are receiving a correct communication. One of the simplest methods is to use a pendulum. If your *'Unihipili* is willing, you can begin. If your *'Unihipili* is not willing, you have to find out why and convince the *'Unihipili* that you love it and want only the best for both of you. Keep reassuring your *'Unihipili* until it cooperates. This may take some time, but be persistent and loving.

**The process is simple!**

Second, invite your *'Aumakua* to be a part of this process. You need its higher wisdom and understanding to make sure you have remastered the skills completely. The *'Aumakua* assists you in moving back into the past to recreate an ideal condition to be able to learn the necessary skills. It has the power to bring you insights you might otherwise overlook. Make this request a formal ceremony so that your *'Unihipili* knows you are serious about this work.

Third, make a commitment to your *'Unihipili,* *'Uhane* and *'Aumakua* that you will complete this process, no matter how long it takes or how difficult it becomes. There are some phases of development that are more difficult to master depending on how long you have been stuck there. This is not a quick fix, but is a permanent way to bring wholeness back into your life.

**You must make a commitment for the process to work.**

Keep a journal of your progress and write down your commitment on the first page. Keep your journal as a sacred record to remind you of your success as a nurturer.

The work consists of reading the sections on the phases of development and noting any feelings or thoughts on that particular phase. It involves discussing the phases with your Inner Selves and deciding whether you have unfinished work at that phase. If you are uncertain, you might have to spend some time in discussion with your *'Unihipili.* Request the memories associated with that age. Take careful note of the emotions and thoughts associated with the memories. The emotional content will give you direction. If you are still uncertain, ask your *'Aumakua* for guidance.

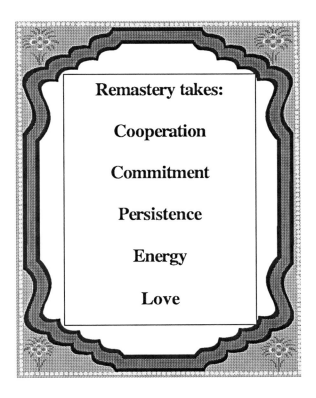

Remastery takes:

Cooperation

Commitment

Persistence

Energy

Love

When you have decided to work on a particular phase, look at the techniques at the end of that section and select the ones to which your *'Unihipili* has an emotional reaction. The fact that there is an emotional reaction indicates you should use that particular exercise. Pay close attention because the *'Unihipili* will try to convince you it is okay, when it really has some problems. Be kind, gentle and understanding and talk out loud to your *'Unihipili* when you explain what the three of you are going to do.

As you progress through each phase, make notes and comments. When you have successfully mastered the skills of a certain level, make a celebration ceremony that involves some tangible item you can display that symbolizes your success. Write down in your journal that you have succeeded and are moving on to the next phase.

Before you study the first phase of development, go back and read the list of self-esteem elements one by one. Pause after each element and make a careful note of any feelings that rise up from the *'Unihipili* or any thoughts that come into your mind from your *'Uhane*. These are clues or insights into areas that need inner work. Use these notes to help you pinpoint the specific phase of development you need to master. Self-esteem is a quality of the *'Unihipili* and you need to listen very carefully to what your *'Unihipili* tells you about its self-esteem. Self-esteem begins at conception and continues throughout life. You can raise your level of self-esteem by mastering the developmental skills.

**BE POSITIVE YOU WILL SUCCEED!**

Be positive that you will succeed and know that you are in exactly the right place moving towards wholeness and a new understanding of the wonderful Selves in your care.   Believe that you will succeed because it is your right to be a whole and perfect!

---

**It is your right to be whole and perfect.**

---

# PRENATAL PHASE OF DEVELOPMENT

## THE INNER SELVES FROM CONCEPTION TO BIRTH

The phase "conception to birth" is not usually included in the study of the development of the human being. It should be because it is a very important phase for us to understand. Using the *Huna* teachings, my own personal observation, experience, and research, I have hypothesized the following explanation of what happens from conception through birth.

According to the ancient *kahuna*, the *'Unihipili* and *'Uhane* are fully intelligent at birth. If that is a fact, then the two Selves are also fully intelligent at conception. Further, the *kahuna* believed that the *'Aumakua* possesses the atom-splitting power of creation and is ever present in the life of the person. Therefore, it is certain that the *'Aumakua* is present at the creation of the new life. The act of conception is an act that combines the intelligence and higher power of all Three High Selves, the *Po'e'Aumakua*, to accomplish.

At the moment of conception, the *Po'e 'Aumakua* of the mother, father, and child come together to create the new physical body—the *kino*. It is the combination of the *mana-loa* or power of all three High Selves that quickens the new life. The *'Aumakua* of the child has already prepared the etheric body (*aka* body) of the *'Unihipili* that is the pattern for the new physical body. The *'Aumakua* has also prepared the *aka* body of the *'Uhane*. These etheric or *aka* bodies are pressed down into the physical plane to house the consciousness of the *'Unihipili* and the *'Uhane*. The *Po'e 'Aumakua* of the three persons involved have already agreed upon the family relationship of the new being and the highest good for the parents and the child.

Male directive Energy

*Female Receptive Energy*

The physical union of the parents is, in reality, a holy, love-filled prayer. I call it the "Sacred Prayer of Union." At its highest level, this prayer involves the masculine and feminine energies; the emotions of the *'Unihipili*; the Will and intention of the *'Uhane*; and, the transforming power of the *Po'e 'Aumakua*. When heightened joy and love are present at such a union, the prayer is sent with a super charge of *mana*. The *mana* expands and flows upward with the prayer to the *Po'e 'Aumakua* waiting on the spiritual plane.

James Redfield, in *Secret of Shambhala: In Search of the Eleventh Insight,* explains the Sacred Prayer of Union as the "…merging of energy fields in a very real way that orgasmically opens a gate into heaven and allows the soul in. The genes of the mother and father combine to make a child whose characteristics are synchronistic with the best destinies of all three people." This is exactly the process as understood through the *Huna* concepts.

As the sperm/energy enters the egg/energy, the extra surcharge of *mana* is transformed by the *Po'e 'Aumakua* into life-creating *mana-loa*, which ignites the spark of life. This could also be described as the moment when God breathes Life into Her child. It is this igniting of the life force that causes the fertilized egg to divide and to continue to divide. A small part of the

**The combined *mana-loa* ignites the spark of life!**

consciousness of the *'Unihipili* of the child flows into the physical plane from the spiritual plane, together with a small part of the newly formed *aka* body. This is the beginning of the formation of the *aka* cord between the child's *'Unihipili* and *'Aumakua*, which will continue to strengthen throughout the lifetime of the child.

From this point until the first flutterings of the body are felt in the womb, the *Po'e 'Aumakua* remain close to the newly developing life. They are deeply involved in the progress of the *kino*. They continue to support, nourish and assist the child's *'Unihipili* throughout the cell development process. They assist the *'Uhane* with its work of developing the neuro-system.

During the next nine months the fetus will grow into the full pattern of the *kino*.  The growth of a human physical body from a single cell-to embryo-to-fetus-to baby is an astounding feat!  Most of this astounding growth happens before the mother is even aware she is pregnant!  Let's look at some of the high points in that growth pattern when the *'Unihipili*, *'Uhane*, and *'Aumakua* are hard at work.

 ## NEONATAL DEVELOPMENT

| | | |
|---|---|---|
| Day 1 | - | Combination of genes from both parents and the first division of the fertilized cell as the *Po'e 'Aumakua* ignite the spark of life. |
| Day 2 | - | Second division of fertilized cell. |
| Day 3 | - | Cells reach a total of 16 or 32. |
| Day 4 | - | Cells total 60-70. |
| Day 5 | - | Embryo enters mother's uterus. *'Unihipili* and *aka* pattern of the body enter the physical plane. *Aka* cord forms between *'Unihipili* and *'Aumakua*. |
| Day 6-9 | - | Embryo attaches to uterus wall. Cells begin to differentiate into layers or kinds of cells to form various elements of the body. |
| Day 10-13 | - | Primitive streak forms which will become spinal cord. Embryo is doubling in size every day. |
| Day 14-17 | - | Umbilical cord and amnion form. |
| Day 18 | - | Nervous system starts to form and for next 10 days will be the focus of growth. *'Uhane* and its *aka* body enter the physical world. Both eyes and ears have formed and are faintly detectable. |
| Day 20 | - | Neuro-system forms. |
| End of 3rd week | - | Brain has formed, including fore-brain, mid-brain and hind-brain. Heart begins to pump. |

## MOTHER MAY SUSPECT SHE IS NOW PREGNANT

| | | |
|---|---|---|
| End of 4th week | - | Embryo is ¼ inch long, weighs less than 2 gram. Morning sickness may occur. |
| End of 5th week | - | Finger outlines have formed along with external ears. Embryo is ½ inch long and is now known as fetus. |
| End of 6th week | - | Muscles are beginning to be controlled by the brain. Fetus is ¾ inch long and weighs 2-3 grams. |

| | | |
|---|---|---|
| End of 7th week | - | Brain is now the focus of growth. Neurons are being added at the rate of **thousands every minute**. |
| End of 2nd month | - | Fetus is capable of responding to touch. |
| End of 3rd month | - | Brain growth continues. Neurons are being added at **thousands every second**. |
| End of 4th month | - | More reflexes developing, including sucking, swallowing, and frowning. Lips begin to protrude. Sheathing of nerve fibers begins. |
| End of 5th month | - | Hiccups occur. Heart beat can be heard externally. Fetus weighs less than 1 lb. Fetus now has **full quota of nerve cells, 12-15 billion**. |
| End of 6th month | - | Fetus weighs 1 lb. 6 oz. It can grip firmly with hands and open and close eyelids. Premature birth is possible, but not ideal. |
| End of 7th month | - | The retinal layer of the eyes is complete and the eye is now light receptive. Fetus gains legal right to be separated from its mother. |
| End of 8th month | - | Weight is now 5 lbs. and growing. |
| End of 9th month | - | Fetus adds 50% of its weight in the final 28 days. Brain appears undoubtedly human. 'Aumakua signals Unihipili to start birthing process. |

# BABY IS READY TO BE BORN

From day 1 through day 17, the 'Aumakua and 'Unihipili are working with the aka pattern of the body. The 'Aumakua is manifesting the body piece by piece. On day 18 when the nervous system begins to form, the 'Uhane enters the body. The 'Aumakua presses a part of the aka body of the 'Uhane into the physical plane to allow it to develop the neuro-system. The brain is the beginning of the neuro-system. By the 6th week the muscles are beginning to be controlled and directed by the 'Uhane. By 5 months, more of the consciousness of the 'Uhane has entered the body and the mother will feel movement within her womb. As more neurons are added, more control over the reflexes is gained. In the 7th month, the eyes become light perceptive and are ready to start receiving input from the environment. The 'Uhane begins the elementary ordering of visual and auditory input. The fetus hears the internal sounds of the mother's body and sees subdued light. The 'Unihipili continues to put weight on the body in readiness for the birth.

Just as the baby is connected to the life-giving mother by the physical umbilical cord, the 'Unihipili and 'Uhane are connected to the life-giving 'Aumakua by a spiritual umbilical cord. Both the Selves can withdraw from the body at any time during the development of the fetus through this spiritual umbilical cord that connects them to the spiritual plane. They will withdraw if a problem develops with the fetus. If this happens, both the Selves will return to the spiritual plane and await the next opportunity to be born. This spiritual umbilical cord closes off naturally at about 3 months after birth, when the *'Unihipili* and *'Aumakua* have strengthened the major *aka* cord. The closing of the fontanels on the baby's skull indicates the spiritual umbilical cord has been sealed off.

About two weeks before the birth, the child's *'Aumakua* determines that the development of the baby in the womb is sufficient for survival and sends a message to the child's *'Unihipili*. The *'Unihipili* activates the hormonal message that chemically signals the mother's *'Unihipili* to begin the birthing sequence. Scientists have recently discovered this chemical signal can be detected in the mother's saliva about two weeks prior to the onset of labor.

> **The *'Aumakua* determines when the baby will be born.**

During the time in the womb and for several weeks afterwards, both the *'Unihipili* and *'Uhane* fluctuate between the world of the physical and the world of the spiritual. They are resting on the spiritual plane from their great body building efforts on the physical plane. The full consciousness of the *'Uhane* enters the body with the first breath of air at birth. The full consciousness of the *'Unihipili* enters the body between 4-6 weeks after the birth. When the baby's eyes clear the *'Unihipili* has fully entered the body.

---

### Developmental Skill of Prenatal Phase

1. **The ability to feel love and acceptance.**

---

The basic skill the Selves learn in this phase of development is being able to feel loved and accepted. This is the only skill to master at this developmental phase, but is the most critical skill. **All other skills are based on this first one.** In the section on "Communication Between the Selves," we discussed how a mother and father communicate psychically with their unborn child. They use the nonverbal methods of feelings, images, sounds, energy and movement. The messages parents send to their unborn child influence the mastery of the prenatal skill of feeling loved and accepted.

# *HUNA* TECHNIQUES FOR MASTERING PRENATAL SKILLS

| **The ability to feel love and acceptance.** |
| --- |

If parents send negative messages to their unborn child, his *'Unihipili* accepts them as his own. His *'Uhane* is not strong enough to interpret the messages as coming from others. The *'Unihipili* will accept messages of being a burden or being unloved or unwelcome as the basic foundation of his life. If the birth is traumatic, similar negative messages will be lodged in the memory of the *'Unihipili*. If you discover emotions or thoughts centered around being unloved or unwelcome into the world, you may need to master this very first skill of feeling love and acceptance.

**The first step is acknowledgement**. Ask your *'Unihipili* to remember the events and feelings surrounding your birth. Spend some time remembering what your mother told you about her pregnancy and your birth. Spend time remembering what your father told you. If you know nothing about your birth, check with your mother or someone else who can tell you about the circumstances. This information gives you clues as to how your *'Unihipili* stored these memories. After discussing the information and feelings about your birth with both your Selves, write down all the feelings and thoughts about your entry into the world. Let the tears come as you remember and write these down. It is sad to feel unloved and unwanted. Grieving is a necessary part of acknowledgement.

**The next step is cleansing and forgiveness**. You must ask your *'Unihipili* to forgive you, the *'Uhane*, for not taking care of it at that time. Explain that the *'Uhane* was just a baby too and not yet strong enough to interpret the messages while you were in the womb. Forgive your mother or father, or whoever sent you those messages. Explain that they did not understand how important it was for you to be welcomed with love. Explain that they did not know what they were doing and how it affected you. Remind your *'Unihipili* that you love it and that your mother and father do love you. Remind your *'Unihipili* that your *'Aumakua*, your Divine Mother and Father, has always loved and wanted you, just as you are. Picture this Divine Love as a beautiful golden light that flows constantly around you. Ask your *'Aumakua* to send a powerful feeling of unlimited love to your *'Unihipili*. Be open to receiving that love. Raise your arms to heaven and take in all this unceasing, unlimited love that has been yours from the beginning. When you feel surrounded and engulfed in this wonderful love, begin the formal forgiveness ceremony.

> **Forgiveness is an important practice to achieve wholeness.**

**Forgiveness Ceremony.** Begin by centering yourself and calming your thoughts and feelings. Take several deep breaths until you feel peaceful. Light a candle to symbolize this is a ceremony. Write down on a piece of paper that you forgive your mother in your own words. Write down on another piece of paper that you forgive your father. Pray for the assistance of your *'Aumakua* in this ceremony of forgiveness. Remain quiet and breathe deeply for a few more minutes to fill yourself with energy. Read your words of forgiveness out loud four times with all the power of forgiveness your *'Uhane* can generate and with all the emotions your *'Unihipili* can bring forth. After the fourth reading of each forgiveness sentence, burn the piece of paper as a symbolic act that you have forgiven each person. While the papers burn release the forgiveness to your *'Aumakua* that it be made manifest in your life.

> **Light a candle to symbolize a formal ceremony.**

Thank your *'Unihipili* and *'Uhane* for their help in this process of forgiveness. Thank your *'Aumakua* for the Divine Love that now fills your heart and mind. Know that you are loved and accepted and welcomed to be in the world. Stay in an attitude of prayer and breathe deeply of forgiveness. End your ceremony with "So it is and ever shall be. *Amama* (Amen in Hawaiian)." Write in your journal that you have forgiven those who unknowingly sent you such negative messages. If you feel any residual emotions over the next few days, read this sentence aloud and remember you are on your way to wholeness.

**Do a reconstruction meditation**. Find a quiet place with soothing and gentle music playing in the background. It is best to do this meditation while lying on the floor wrapped securely and warmly in a soft blanket. Close your eyes and take several deep breaths while centering yourself and relaxing your mind and emotions and your physical body. Now imagine a time when you were in the womb. Feel yourself very small in a warm, dark and very safe place. You feel cozy and surrounded by love. Picture your ideal mother and father in each other's arms sending their love to you. Stay in this place for a few minutes taking in all their love. Now imagine your tiny body pushing out of the womb and emerging into the light of the world. Stretch your arms and legs and move like a newborn. Open your eyes a tiny bit and see the hazy outlines of all the loving adults present at your

> **We can reconstruct an ideal situation for our Selves by going back and rewriting the script of our lives.**

birth. Listen to their gentle voices and feel their gentle caresses. Feel the loving arms of your ideal mother holding you close as she nestles you to her breast. Find her warm and comforting nipple and take it in your tiny mouth and begin to suck. Pucker your lips and make them move in a sucking motion. Suck on her nipple and take in all the love you can hold. Stay in this place of comfort and love for as long as you want. There is no hurry to break away. You can have all the love and comforting you need.

When you feel fully satisfied with love and comfort, slowly release your mother's nipple and be contented. Stay in this contentment for as long as you want. When you are ready, take a deep breath and begin to return to the present. Take your time to return; there is no hurry. Take a few deep breaths and reactivate your physical body in the present. Know that you can return to this place of love and comfort whenever you want. It is the place of genuine love of your Holy

Mother, for it is her arms that have held you close to her heart. It is her love that has comforted and nurtured you. Take another deep breath and slowly open your eyes to a new world, secure in the knowledge that you are welcome and loved. You were born in love and you remain in love. (You can record this reconstruction meditation and play it for yourself or have someone you trust read it for you as you do the exercise.)

Create a new welcome for yourself. Write a special letter of welcome on baby stationary or a new baby card to your 'Unihipili saying all of the welcoming words you would like to hear at your birth. Here are some suggestions:

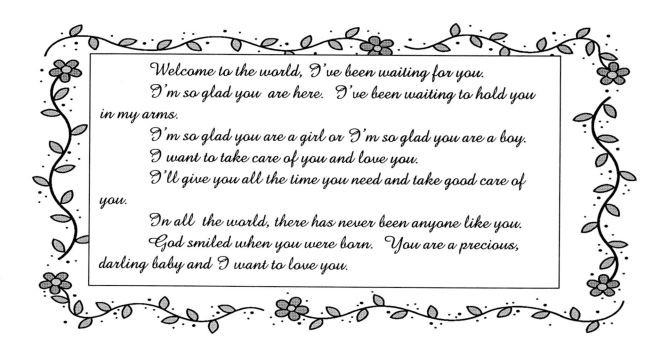

*Welcome to the world, I've been waiting for you.*

*I'm so glad you are here. I've been waiting to hold you in my arms.*

*I'm so glad you are a girl or I'm so glad you are a boy.*

*I want to take care of you and love you.*

*I'll give you all the time you need and take good care of you.*

*In all the world, there has never been anyone like you. God smiled when you were born. You are a precious, darling baby and I want to love you.*

Include a picture of yourself as a baby or cut a newborn picture out of a magazine. Include any other symbols that would make you feel welcome. Sign the letter, "Your Loving and Eternal Mother." Then mail the letter to yourself. When you receive it, read it out loud to your 'Unihipili. Feel the joy of being welcomed to the world. Put the letter in your journal as a keepsake to remind you that **you are loved**!

# THE DEVELOPMENTAL PHASE OF INFANCY

## THE INNER SELVES FROM BIRTH TO TWO YEARS

No other period in a person's life evolves as rapidly and contains such dramatic changes as these first two years of life. The phase of development known as Infancy spans the period from newborn to 24 months or 2 years of age. The period spent in the womb is the most accelerated time of <u>physical </u>growth. Scientists now recognize that as much, if not more, growth and development occur **after** birth than before. Infancy is the most accelerated time of <u>mental</u> and <u>emotional</u> growth. It has been only within the last 30 years that we have realized the incredible importance of this phase of development.

Barbara and Philip Newman, early childhood specialists, state, "The study of perceptual development during infancy has revealed that infants know the world or respond to differences in the environment with much more sensitivity and selectiveness than we had previously

> **The mastery of all future skills begins in Infancy.**

imagined." The **mastery of all future skills** begins here in infancy. The *'Unihipili* and *'Uhane* are fully intelligent when they are born into the body. Infancy is the time when the *'Unihipili* learns to use the physical body and transmit information gathered through the senses to the *'Uhane*. The *'Uhane* learns to organize and interpret the information; develop the conceptualization process; develop higher reasoning abilities; and, learn how to control and direct the activities of the two Selves.

Once the *'Unihipili* is no longer confined to a small enclosed space, it can accelerate the physical growth of the body, begin to use the physical senses to give information to the *'Uhane,* and store the memories. As soon as the *'Uhane* is finished refining the neuro-circuits of the brain and nervous system, it can begin to process this information and categorize it. Both consciousnesses begin to work together as they master the control of the physical body and then interact with the environment.

> **Human beings are explorers here to master the world.**

I like to think of human beings as explorers. Our physical body is the vehicle for exploration. Our two minds work together to construct the vehicle and then use it to explore this wonderful world of Planet Earth. However, it takes time to learn control and to develop the necessary motor skills (physical skills). It also takes time for the Selves to learn to live together and with the other explorers (emotional and social skills). It takes time to learn language and conceptualization (intellectual skills). **Why, it takes us almost three years!!! In the space of 36 months our wonderfully talented and highly intelligent Inner Selves have mastered the world!**

There are certain skills each Infant must learn in order to move on the next phase of development. These tasks are best learned by the *'Uhane* and *'Unihipili* of the child without any outside interference, but they need the support and love of their parents.

---

### Developmental Skills of Infancy

1. **The development of social attachment. This is the cornerstone for inner and outer personal relationships. (*'Unihipili* skill)**

2. **The development of the sense of the permanence of objects. This is the basis for the development of logical thinking. (*'Uhane* skill)**

3. **The development of the understanding of means-ends relationships. (*'Unihipili* and *'Uhane* skills)**

4. **The development of primary motor functions. These functions are directed functions of eye-hand, reaching, sitting, crawling, standing, and walking. The mastery of these skills gives us the fundamental competence to master the environment. (*'Uhane* and *'Unihipili* skills)**

---

Jean Piaget, the famous Swiss psychologist, called his understanding of this early learning, "cognitive theory." He believed that from birth to 18 months a child developed "increasingly complex sensory and motor patterns, which allow the infant to organize and more adequately control his environment." These sensorimotor skills are mastered through investigation and perception of the infant's environment. These acts build concepts. With repetition and experimentation they form the "laws" of predictable sequences.

The first skill is learned during the first 5 weeks of life. The 'Unihipili learns about personal relationships based on the nurturing care and closeness of his mother. This is called the mother/infant bond. This social and emotional relationship builds the foundation for all subsequent relationships, including friendships and marriages. It is our foundation for trust. Without trust we cannot become independent and move out to explore on our own. This first task also builds the foundation for trust and love between the child's two Selves.

The second developmental skill is reaching for and grasping an object. This important skill is the basis for all subsequent intellectual learning. This skill is acquired at about age 4-6 months. It is fascinating to me that by mastering the skill of reaching out and grasping an object we learn everything else. This simple act is symbolic of the intricacies of the two minds and the cooperative actions of the Inner Selves. What a marvelous team of Selves we have!

> **By reaching and grasping, we learn everything else.**

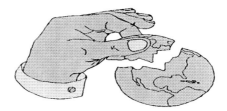

The period beginning at age 6 months, when the child begins to manipulate objects, is the beginning of our understanding of the physical laws of the earth. The child learns through experimentation and repetition the certain laws of cause and effect. We have to learn these laws in order to move our vehicle, or body, around in the environment. This developmental skill must be learned by both the 'Unihipili and the 'Uhane.

The fourth skill is the development of the motor functions. These include the ability to see something and reach out with the hand to grasp it; to sit the body upright; to move the body unaided by first crawling and then walking; and then to refine these locomotive skills. This is a skill that takes the cooperation of both Inner Selves to master.

The most critical developmental skill begins at birth with the formation of the loving and strong mother/infant bond. The second most critical phase begins at 8 months. This is the time when the child begins to physically move about alone. She becomes a mobile explorer. Burton L. White, M.D., in his book, *The First Three Years of Life*, states that "the greatest opportunity parents have to influence their children for a lifetime is through the quality of their interaction during the period from 8 and 24 months."

Infancy is a crucial time in the lives of the Selves. They are continuing the development of the physical body and the neuro-circuits they began in the womb. As soon as the vehicle for exploration is complete, the two Selves begin to manipulate it by learning how to move and control the head, neck, arms, hands, legs, and feet. Once they can control the parts, they use them to turn the body over and begin to move independently. As the physical development continues, so does the emotional and mental. All other skills we learn are based on the foundational skills we learn during Infancy.

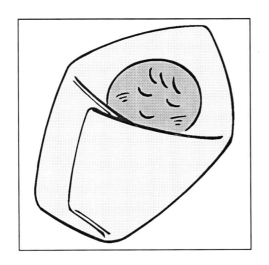

# THE INNER SELVES
# AS THE NEWBORN

Babies enter the world fresh from a State of Love. The *'Aumakua* is ever present throughout the process of creating and building the new human body. The *'Aumakua* facilitates the moving of the consciousness of the *'Uhane* and *'Unihipili* into the body. Then the *'Aumakua* moves to its normal position, a slight distance away but still connected by the *aka* cord to the other Selves. Shortly after birth a "veil of forgetfulness" descends on the *'Uhane* and *'Unihipili*. You can observe this phenomenon in all newborns. For up to 60 minutes after birth a newborn's eyes are clear and full of intelligence. The newborn looks around at her surroundings and at her parents, as if remembering, then the veil drops and the eyes become hazy and blurred. They clear up again at about age two months when the *'Unihipili* is fully present in the body.

The newborn sleeps most of the time, waking only to eat or if he is uncomfortable. During this sleeping time, the consciousnesses of the *'Uhane* and *'Unihipili* return to the spiritual realm for renewal, leaving a part of their consciousness in the newborn to keep the body and mind working. The newborn will only be alert for an average of 3 minutes per hour during the day or night. Over the next two months this alert time will increase to 6-7 minutes per hour. The *'Uhane* and *'Unihipili* are resting from their labors. This should also be a time for rest for the mother. Giving birth is exhausting for everyone. This is a time for recuperation, for quiet, peace and serenity.

Beginning from the moment of conception, the newborn's *'Unihipili* is registering impressions and storing them as blueprints for future reference. Each time a person handles, talks to, comforts, feeds, or is in the presence of the newborn, an impression is being formed and stored. Daniel Goleman states that "...every interaction, no matter how small, is making an imprint on the newborn child. These are stored as 'blueprints' for his emotional life." We want these impressions, these blueprints, to be positive.

The care of the newborn Selves centers around feeding and changing. It is important to handle the newborn in a gentle and tranquil manner. His 'Unihipili is highly sensitive to bright lights and loud noises. The newborn just came from a muffled and dim world and loud noises and bright lights are too much for his new eyes and ears. Newborns respond better in a quiet, dimly lit room. Newborns are also highly sensitive to space. They prefer the same secure closeness they had in the womb. Newborns should be wrapped snugly in a receiving blanket for the first several weeks of life, which gives them that safe and secure feeling.

Smiles are sometimes seen flitting across the faces of newborns. There are many stories to explain this phenomenon. Since the 'Uhane is not strong enough to control the face muscles, I believe these smiles are glimpses of joy and delight sent to the parents by the child's 'Aumakua from the world of Spirit.

The newborn Selves are seemingly helpless, but that is not the truth. They are able to breathe, root, mouth, suck, frown, sneeze, swallow, salivate, cry, smell, taste, hear, yawn, hiccup, cough and stretch. They do have very weak necks and shoulders. The head must be supported at all

**Newborns are not helpless.**

times until it gains strength. When a newborn is placed in a prone position on her stomach, she can usually lift her head high enough to avoid suffocation. Her hands and feet can grasp objects, if someone else helps. She can hang onto your finger with a surprising strength measured at 2 lbs. of pulling power. She loses this enormous strength in a few months.

A newborn can glance at an object, in his alert state, that is large and contrasts well with the background and is no closer than 6-8 inches. He has a startle response that disappears at about three months. This response is triggered if his body is rapidly lowered through space, if he hears a sharp noise, or if he sees a bright light turned on suddenly in a dim room. It also happens during sleep. This startle reaction is similar to the adult startle experience, when the body jerks awake from a light sleep. This startle reflex is a physical response to the 'Unihipili suddenly being pulled back into the body by these stimuli.

Newborns have a surprising walking reflex. When supported upright under their arms they will move their legs and feet in a "walking" manner. We don't know why the human newborn is able to do this. Newborns can also propel their bodies if they are unhappy or uncomfortable. Some newborns mysteriously fall off of beds or other seemingly safe places.

Jean Piaget in his landmark book, *Origins of Intelligence*, says that a baby's behavior at birth consists of a small number of "somewhat clumsy, unfinished, isolated reflexes." Piaget believed that the reflexes of rooting, sucking, grasping, and occasionally glancing are the "foundation elements of all later intelligence." He also believed that these behaviors are "ancient fragments of what long ago made up useful, organized, instinctive patterns."

If we look at these behaviors through *Huna*, we see them as rudimentary reflexes used by the 'Unihipili to control the new body. Most of these newborn reflexes were mastered in the womb. Through the refinement of these basic reflexes the 'Unihipili will gain complete control of the physical body. The *'Uhane* meanwhile is building and directing the neuro-circuits of the brain and nervous system to enable it to direct such reflexes in a conscious manner.

The newborn Selves are interested in only one thing – simple comfort. They prefer to be fed when hungry and changed when dirty or wet. They desire peace, serenity and quiet. Both Selves are resting and recuperating from a long arduous ordeal. It is interesting to note that when adults are distressed or overly active, that peace, serenity and quiet soothe and comfort them just as they did when the Selves were newly born. The favorite condition of the newborn is sleeping. In this sleep the Selves are resting and renewing mind, body, emotions, and spirit. Newborns desire to be held and to feel close to their mothers at all times. Parts of the nervous system are activated when a baby is picked up and held closely. That is why newborns are designed to be cuddled, caressed and moved "gently through space."

---

### Developmental Skills of the Newborn

1. **The establishment of the mother/infant bond. (*'Unihipili* skill)**

2. **The ability to respond promptly to needs and discomfort.
( *'Uhane* skill)**

---

This is the time of establishing the important mother/infant bond. The mother does this by keeping the newborn as close to her as possible at all times. Western mothers are in close contact with their babies only 25% of the time compared to mothers of other cultures, who keep their babies with them constantly. The newborn Selves need the closeness of their mother because they are continuing to develop the physical body and neuro-systems. They spent the first nine months inside the mother's body and they need to spend the next nine months as close to her body as possible for optimum development.

Bonding means "the formation of a close personal relationship especially through frequent or constant association." (*The Merriam-Webster Dictionary*) Good bonding with his primary caretaker is critical to the development of every human being. We are now just beginning to understand how important this mother/infant bond really is. The best bonding occurs

> **Good bonding forms the foundation for all other relationships.**

with the breast nurturer, his mother. She is biologically designed for this work. Good bonding forms the foundation for all other relationships and also forms the foundation for self-esteem, emotional health, intelligence, love and trust.

Tine Thevenin believes that we need "all the love we can get, and especially a mother's inherent love at the very beginning: a love that holds us close but is prepared to let go; a love that is given for the benefit of the child, not for the mother's own benefit." As this strong, intimate bond develops, a mother comes to know her child's wants, needs, moods and feelings. An old Jewish proverb says, "A mother understands what her child does not say." The mother/infant bond benefits both mother and child.

This is also true of the bond between the Selves. A *'Uhane* that constantly controls the emotions of the *'Unihipili* is not demonstrating love. Neither is a *'Unihipili* who always insists on its own emotional way. We learn about love first from our mothers. The mother represents the mothering aspects of the *'Aumakua* to the newly born Selves. They depend on her to take

> **The bond between the Selves is beneficial to all three.**

care of them and protect them during this critical time of rest and recuperation. To feel her constant presence in the form of her physical body reminds them of the constant presence of the *'Aumakua*.

The *'Uhane* and *'Unihipili* are 'closely intertwined," according to Max Freedom Long. Because the newborn's *'Uhane* is unable to take active control, the child's *'Unihipili* comes to

> **The newborn believes his mother's *'Uhane* is his own.**

believe his mother's *'Uhane* is his other Self. He is not aware that they are separate human beings. This awareness of separateness begins at about age 2 when the child's own *'Uhane* is strong enough to begin to exert control and to experiment with its Will. Until that time the child will continue to rely on his mother's *'Uhane* to fill in. This is the reason the child believes his mother is an extension of himself.

The second most critical element for a newborn is to respond promptly to his cries or discomfort. Meeting needs is part of bonding. Dr. Burton White explains that, in his judgment, "giving the infant a feeling of being loved and cared for is...the single most important goal in getting a child off to a good start in life." Recent research has proven that the basic foundation of a child's personality is being formed in his earliest interchanges with nurturing adults. These interchanges are the responses to the newborn's cries.

Depending on how his needs are met, the newborn's *'Unihipili* also makes his first judgment of the world, on which all other judgments are based. To make a judgment is to form an opinion after discerning and comparing. Is his new world to be trusted or mistrusted? This basic belief is difficult to overcome later in life, whether the belief is one of trust or mistrust.

> **The cry of an infant or child or *'Unihipili* should never go unanswered!**

"The crying of an infant or young child should **never** go unanswered," states Thevenin. The newborn only knows he is not comfortable and that "anxiety fills the whole moment and the moment is without end." This is a good description of the basic feeling of the *'Unihipili*. Since the emotional mind is the strongest mind in the newborn, all feelings are intense.

The *'Uhane* of the newborn, although fully intelligent, cannot yet talk, nor can it exercise any kind of control over the *'Unihipili*. The neuro-circuits of the brain and nervous system have not developed sufficiently. Nor has the *'Uhane* learned how to use its Will to direct actions and thoughts. That will come later. You could say that a newborn is 99% *'Unihipili* and 1% *'Uhane*.

This developmental skill of prompt responding is a good point to remember as we nurture our Inner Selves. A cry from the *'Unihipili* should never go unanswered by the *'Uhane*. Whatever is bothering our *'Unihipili* fills the here and now, and we must respond as soon as possible. We have all experienced the nagging anxiety of our *'Unihipili* when he or she is bothered by something. This anxiety colors everything we think, say, or do. It lodges in the pit of our stomach. And we have all experienced the great feeling of relief when we have resolved the problem.

Infants experience the world differently from adults. They have a great capacity to shift moods abruptly. This very moment is the most important moment. There is no awareness of time or space or separateness. Time and space, which are organizational constructs of the *'Uhane*, are not understood by the *'Unihipili*. Learning control of the new physical body from the inside, the newborn *'Unihipili* needs someone else to direct the care from the outside. When the child is older, his own *'Uhane* will direct that care. Until then, the mother must stand in as the child's *'Uhane* and direct the care of the physical body and care for the emotions of the newborn *'Unihipili*.

The newborn Selves need rest, feeding and changing. They need breast nurturing from their mothers and being held next to her body as much as possible. Parents should respond to the newborn's needs immediately. The way in which newborn Inner Selves are treated in these first crucial weeks lays the foundation for their view of the world, their ability to learn, the state of their emotional and physical health, and their future relationships. This newborn phase of development is the foundation of all other phases.

# *HUNA* TECHNIQUES FOR MASTERING THE NEWBORN SKILLS

In the prenatal phase of development, the skill of feeling loved and welcomed was the only developmental skill to master. In the newborn phase there are two skills to master. We use acknowledgement, forgiveness, reconstruction, and ritual to reclaim these skills.

 | **The establishment of the mother/infant bond.**

If you experience any emotions of thoughts centered around the issues of being close to your mother and being unconditionally accepted by her, you have not yet mastered the skill of the mother/infant bond.

**The first step is acknowledgement**. Ask your *'Unihipili* to remember events and feelings of the first few weeks of your life. Talk with your mother and/or father and other people, who might have information about that time. Find out what was going on and the feelings of your at that time. Spend some time discussing the circumstances and feelings about yourself as a newborn with your two Selves. Write down all the feelings and thoughts. Let the tears come to help cleanse way any feelings of separation from your mother, of not feeling her warmth and love. Grieving is a necessary part of acknowledgement.

**The next step is forgiveness.** Review the forgiveness ceremony in the prenatal technique section. Ask your *'Unihipili* to forgive you for not being strong enough to provide you with comfort and closeness. Then forgive your mother for not knowing what you needed, for being unaware of the importance of holding you close during this critical time of your life. Remind your *'Unihipili* that your mother loves you and has always loved you. She is a reflection of the Holy Mother. Remind your *'Unihipili* that your *'Uhane* loves it unconditionally. Ask your Holy Mother, your *'Aumakua*, to be present and fill you with warmth and love. Picture the Golden Light of Love flowing all around you. Ask your *'Unihipili* to receive this Golden Light of Love. Raise your arms to heaven and take in all the love and closeness you can hold.

When you are feeling centered and filled with love, light a candle and take two pieces of small rope in your hands. One piece represents your mother and the other piece represents you. Ask the *'Aumakua* to bless these two pieces of rope that will be rejoined. Tie them together with great ceremony and say out loud with great emotion:

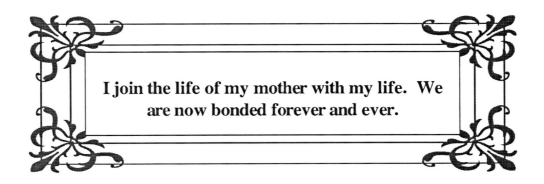

I join the life of my mother with my life. We are now bonded forever and ever.

Picture your mother standing in the Light of her *'Aumakua*. Picture you standing in the Light of your *'Aumakua*. Embrace your mother and merge the sacred Lights together. Be in the arms of your mother and hold her in your arms. Know that you are bonded in Spirit. Thank your mother and thank her *'Aumakua*. Thank your *'Unihipili* and your *'Uhane*. Thank your *'Aumakua*. Stay in the attitude of prayer for a few minutes breathing deeply and being forgiving. End your ceremony with "So it is and ever shall be. *Amama*."

Write in your journal that you have forgiven your mother and rejoined the bond between you. Carry your joined rope close to your body for the next 30 days to remind you of this bonding. Place it on your personal altar after this time.

**Do a reconstruction meditation**. Go to your meditation place. Take a warm, soft blanket and a cuddly stuffed animal with you. Play soothing music softly in the background. Wrap your body in the blanket and cradle the stuffed animal in your arms. Close your eyes and breathe deeply to get centered. Imagine a time when you were newly arrived in the world. Picture yourself as a newborn, soft delicate skin, tiny fingers and toes, tiny body sleeping in a warm blanket. Listen to your ideal mother's gentle voice as she picks you up and holds you close to her heart. Feel the gentle rhythm of her body as she sits down in her rocking chair and begins to rock. Take a deep breath and smell her womanly fragrance. Move your body in a rocking motion and feel safe, loved and secure in this gentle movement energy. Snuggle into your mother's arms and stay there for as long as you want. There is no hurry to do anything else, just be close to your ideal mother. When you are ready, open your tiny newborn eyes and see the beautiful face of your Holy Mother holding you. Her eyes are full of love as she gazes into yours. It is your Holy Mother, your ideal mother, that keeps you safe, protects you, and loves you. It is to this Holy Mother that you are truly bonded. The world is a safe and loving place for you. Take another deep breath and begin to return your body to the present. Remember you can always return to this moment of perfect love and trust. You are bonded in love and you remain always in love. **You are special and unique and you are loved.**

**Celebrate** your bonding with your Holy Mother and your earthly mother. Give yourself a Bonding Party. Invite a few of your closest friends and their mothers to come. (A substitute mother is welcome also.) Send out fancy invitations or better still, make them yourself. Ask the women to dress up in hats and gloves and the men to wear suits and ties. Serve finger foods and tea and coffee (no alcohol). Share funny stories about the mother/child experiences and enjoy them with laughter. At the end of the party, gather in a circle and give thanks for the mothers and their children. Present each child with 2 flowers, one to give his or her mother, and one to keep. End with a group hug and expressions of love. Take a photograph of every one who attended your bonding party and put it in your journal.

 | **The ability to respond promptly to needs and discomfort.**

If you have emotions or thoughts centered around being accepted and/or not trusting other people or the world, you may need to master this important newborn skill of trust.

**The first step is acknowledgment.** Use the technique described above. Feel the sadness of not being heard. Feel the anger at not being respected. Feel the loneliness of crying all by yourself with no one to hear or care. Grieve and let the tears flow. No cry of any infant or child should go unanswered.

**The next step is forgiveness.** Follow the forgive process as outlined previously. Ask your *'Unihipili* to forgive you for not being strong enough to respond to and answer your early needs. Forgive your mother for not answering your cries and taking care of your needs. Forgive your mother for not understanding how important it was to answer your cries. Do a candle lighting ceremony and ask your *'Aumakua* to help you in this forgiveness process.

For the next 28 days, promise that you will listen carefully to your *'Unihipili*. Listen for any quiet thoughts, reminders, or gentle nudges of realization. Ask your *'Unihipili* to communicate a little stronger so that you will not miss any requests. Stop whatever you are doing and listen carefully. Acknowledge you have heard and repeat the message out loud to make sure you understand it correctly. Your *'Unihipili* might remind you to call someone, or when it is lunchtime, or when it is time to change tasks. Pay close attention to any message with emotional content. Do your best to answer and respond to <u>all</u> the messages. If you are unable to respond immediately, explain out loud to your *'Unihipili* why you cannot respond at that moment. Tell your *'Unihipili* how and when you will respond. **Follow through and do what you have promised.** Every evening for the next 28 days, take some time to review the days events with your *'Unihipili*. Discuss ways in which the *'Uhane* responded to the cries and needs of your *'Unihipili*. By the end of the 28 day period, you will have established a good communication system with your *'Unihipili*. Remember you must keep your promise to listen and respond.

These are the responsibilities of the *'Uhane* throughout life. Your mother was only a substitute *'Uhane* until yours grew strong enough to take over. It is your responsibility now.

**Do a Reconstruction Meditation**. See yourself crying as a newborn and your ideal mother coming to pick you up, holding you and comforting you. See her changing your diapers, feeding you, holding and rocking you. Know that your Holy Mother answers each and every request for assistance and help. Imagine that all of your needs and discomforts are being answered, right now.

**Do a ritual.** On a piece of elegant stationary write a commitment letter from your *'Uhane* to your *'Unihipili*. This letter is a written form of your inner desire and pledge to listen to each and every cry of your own *'Unihipili*. It is a promise to respond promptly and take care of each need. Put this letter of commitment in your journal. Make a note that you have forgiven your mother and yourself for each and every past inaction.

# THE INNER SELVES
# AT FOUR WEEKS

Four weeks marks the beginning of the next phase of development. When the Selves reach the age of four weeks they are able to stay alert longer, up to 6-7 minutes per hour. The eyes have cleared and are able to focus better. Faces become more interesting and the *'Unihipili* will spend some time focusing on them. The region of the face that most interests him is between the hairline and the eyes, especially the eyes. It is no accident that an infant *'Unihipili* focuses first on the eyes. Dr. Joseph Murphy in his book, *The Amazing Laws of Cosmic Mind Power*, says that the eyes are symbolic of Divine Love. "Your right eye symbolizes right thought and right action. The left eye symbolizes God's love and wisdom." The infant Selves recognize the Divine Spirit within the mother and father, shining through their eyes.

The four week old infant Selves need an abundance of breast nurturing and holding. Physically the body is a little stronger. The head still needs support. The arms and legs will begin to move in rhythm to voices. The most active muscles of an infant are those of his mouth and eyes. In fact, at this phase of development, the eyes are more advanced than the hands. The Selves will be eating and sleeping on a more regular schedule. The Selves begin to show interest in the rest of the world.

At four weeks the full consciousness of the *'Unihipili* is residing in the body. It has sufficiently recovered from the rigors of building the new body and from the birth itself. The *'Unihipili* begins to transmit the tastes, smells, sounds, sights, textures and feelings of the outside world to the *'Uhane*. The full consciousness of the *'Uhane* is also residing in the body, centered around the head and brain region. The *'Uhane* begins to organize the sensory signals from the *'Unihipili* into a coherent reality, as it activates the neo-cortex for the first time. The neo-cortex is the seat of thought in the brain. It contains the centers that connect and comprehend what the senses perceive. It is the center for abstract thinking. For instance, it enables the *'Uhane* to put together the act of bonding with the abstraction of love.

The emotional areas of the brain, the limbic system, are so intertwined with the neo-cortex that the *'Unihipili* retains an immense power to influence behavior. The limbic system is the first to develop and kicks in before our thoughts or the neo-cortex takes over. This is an important fact to remember in nurturing our Inner Selves. The emotional mind is always the first responder. The feelings of the *'Unihipili* are the first basic response to any situation and can control our behavior before the *'Uhane* can take action. As a *'Uhane* we have to pay close attention to what is happening at any given time. This is an element of Goleman's EQ, in which we learn how to control the emotional impulses.

---

### Developmental Skills at Four Weeks

1. The ability to focus the eyes and to clearly see. (*'Unihipili* and *'Uhane* skills)

2. The ability to learn by association. (*'Unihipili* skill)

3. The ability to smile in response to stimuli. (*'Uhane* skill)

---

Ivan Pavlov, the famous Russian psychologist, proposed that conceptual development occurs during infancy in the first to six months of life. He believed that conceptual development must come before the development of controlled motor skills. This means that the *'Uhane* must be able **to conceptualize** an action before the *'Unihipili* can control the body **to perform** the action. The *'Uhane* learns to conceptualize by observation. The *'Uhane* spends several weeks just observing. At age four weeks, the *'Uhane* begins this process of active observation. The first observations are those of the mother's face and the faces of other family members.

Pavlov also believed that learning by association is the first basic conceptual development. We use this basic skill for the rest of our lives. Pavlov called this "conditioned learning." Most of the learning of the *'Unihipili* comes from association. For example, in associative learning we automatically stop at all red lights or we get hungry when we smell certain odors. We have learned this behavior through association. The *'Unihipili* files our memories by association rather than by logical order. The *kahuna* used the symbol of a cluster of grapes or a cluster of berries to explain how memories are stored together. Each *'Unihipili* is unique in storing memories by its own association.

**Our memories are stored by association.**

The four week old infant is not only beginning to observe the physical aspects of the faces around her, but is also listening to the expression of feelings. She is listening to the attitudes and tones of voices. She is beginning to conceptualize expression with mood, attitude and sound. All of this input is stored as associative memory and is another element of Golemans' EQ. The ability to understand what another person is feeling comes from this process of conceptualizing feelings.

Sometime from 4-6 weeks the newborn will begin to smile in response to you. This is the first conscious movement directed by the *'Uhane*. It is the simplest form of conscious communication. Some people believe that the first smile is the true birth moment. Others believe the first conscious smile marks the point when the baby matures from fetus to infant. I believe the first conscious smile indicates that the neo-cortex has been activated by the *'Uhane* and the important process of conceptualization has begun.

The infant Selves are now alert and ready to begin interacting with the environment. The *'Unihipili* is making and storing memories by association. The *'Uhane* is beginning to conceptualize by actively observing eyes and interpreting sound.

# *HUNA* TECHNIQUES FOR MASTERING THE FOUR WEEK OLD SKILLS

> **The ability to focus the eyes and clearly see.**

If you have emotions or thoughts centering around your ability to look people straight in the eye (unless it is against your cultural behavior), or seeing people clearly as children of God or Spirit, you may need to master this first skill of the four week old infant.

**Acknowledgement**. Acknowledge out loud that you look away from people's eyes when they look at you. Acknowledge that you don't always see the Divine in every person. Acknowledge your desire to see more clearly now.

**Forgiveness**. Ask your *'Unihipili* to forgive you for not understanding that the "eyes are the windows of the soul." Ask forgiveness out loud from all those people you have "hurt" by not seeing them clearly as children of God. Perform a forgiveness ceremony. After you light the candle, take your mirror and look yourself straight in the eyes and say:

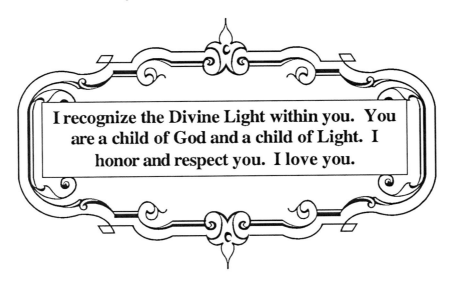

I recognize the Divine Light within you. You are a child of God and a child of Light. I honor and respect you. I love you.

Say this four times to see yourself more clearly and in remembrance of all those people you did not see clearly. Practice seeing the Divine within each person.

**Reconstruction Meditation.** This is an ongoing process. Ask your *'Unihipili* to remember a person and a situation in which you did not see him or her clearly. Reconstruct the same situation using your imagination and this time respond in a different manner. Respond with honor and respect. Continue to do this meditation with **all** the people you have not seen clearly. You only have to reconstruct one situation per person. Write down the name of the person in your journal to remind yourself that you now see them clearly as a child of Spirit. Be careful with your words about this person. Do not say, think, or act other than in Divine order.

**Ritual.** Practice seeing the Divine in the faces of everyone you meet, whether you know them or not. Keep looking at the face until it begins to glow and you can recognize the Divine Light. This is a good exercise to practice with people who are having difficulties or sending out negative emotions. Hold that person in the Light for a few minutes and then release them to their highest good.

 **The ability to learn by association.**

If you discover emotion or thoughts centering around memory, you may need to master the skill of associative learning. Many people are visual learners, some are auditory learners and some are tactile learners. If you are having trouble remembering things visually, you may have a dominant auditory or tactile mode of remembering. In other words, your memories are stored by sound or texture, rather than visually. It is easy to figure out which mode is your dominant mode. Ask your *'Unihipili* to help you remember how you learn. Think back to school and a time when you were listening to a lecture from a teacher. Did you spend more time taking notes or more time listening? If you took notes you probably have a visual associative memory. If you preferred to listen, you probably have auditory or tactile associative memory. There is no wrong way to store memories. Your task is to figure out which way your *'Unihipili* stores them.

Listen to your own words when you are talking to someone. Do you use the auditory words such as "I hear what you are saying?" Or do you say "I feel it would be better to...?" These words give you clues to your associative memory system. You might ask someone else to listen to you and give you feedback. When you ascertain your remembering mode, it will be easy to recall memories from your *'Unihipili*.

**The ability to smile in response to stimuli.**

If you have emotions or thoughts centering around your ability to smile, you may need to master this last skill of the four week old infant. In these modern days of stress, we don't respond often enough with a smile. Put hand-drawn pictures of smiley faces around the house, in your car, and at work as gentle reminders to smile. Ask your *'Unihipili* to help you remember to smile. Smile while standing in line, driving down the highway, reading a book, and while meditating and praying. Respond with a smile when you meet another's eyes. Respond with a smile in negative situations. Smile at yourself in the mirror while you are combing your hair. Find new opportunities to smile in your daily life. Soon you will have mastered this important skill of smiling. It just takes practice.

# THE INNER SELVES AT SIX WEEKS

An infant relies on his parents for nurturing, warmth, consistency and stimulation. Pavlov states that the infant, at this age, is "now conceptualizing the activities of the physical world in order to apply them to the developing physical body." The Selves at six weeks continue the observation and conceptualization process. The *'Unihipili* is sending the sensory signals to the *'Uhane,* who is building the constructs in the neo-cortex in order to conceptualize.

Physically at age six weeks the body is much stronger. The infant begins to hold her hands aloft, but doesn't really see them or use them. She still can't focus her eyes on close objects. The eyes won't be ready for "refined three-dimensional vision" until the age of three months. The infant begins to make cooing noises now, but the throat, tongue and voice box have not fully developed. The baby's cooing aids in this development. Cooing will continue for several months in preparation for speaking. The *'Uhane* and *'Unihipili* are working closely to develop the physical elements necessary for speech.

---

### Developmental Skills for Six Weeks

1. **The ability to conceptualize.  ( *'Uhane* skill )**

2. **The ability to respond to new stimuli.  ( *'Unihipili* and *'Uhane* skills )**

3. **The ability to separate.  ( *'Unihipili* skill )**

---

The environment for learning for the first 5-6 years is the home. The infant Selves generally get all the stimulation they need for their limited activities just being around the family. The Selves like to be carried around by the mother or father and sit where they can observe the family's activities. When the infant is included in the family's normal activities, the Selves have the best opportunity for observation and conceptualization. It is through consistent observation that the *'Uhane* is able to conceptualize.

In *Development Through Life*, authors and psychologists Barbara and Philip Newman state that "...perception and investigation of the environment build concepts." They believe that the "integration of crude responses and diverse stimuli into coordinated and meaningful patterns of behavior..." is critical to the development of the child. It is the responsibility of a good parent to provide such stimuli. The Newmans also believe that the "absence of important environmental characteristics, such as adequate sensory stimulation or responsible care giving can cause a disruption in the developmental process, which will be difficult, if not impossible, to compensate for in later life." As nurturers of our Inner Selves we are responsible to provide adequate sensory stimulation. If we do not provide it, the developmental process will be disrupted. This has ramifications for adult Inner Selves as well. Adequate stimulation is what keeps us growing and learning. Unfortunately, we don't always provide new learning opportunities for our Inner Selves. Instead we watch TV or play video games, two very disruptive stimuli. Our curious and insatiable Inner Selves thrive on new learning experiences.

> **Adequate stimulation is what keeps us going and growing.**

We must provide educational opportunities for the developing Selves. We provide these opportunities and then step back and let the Selves explore and engage in repetition for as long as they desire without interference. Learning is a personal process that is accomplished by each *'Uhane* and *'Unihipili* independently. This is true for the Selves at six weeks and true for the Selves at any other age. Learning is the process of intelligence utilizing a moveable vehicle in order to explore its environment.

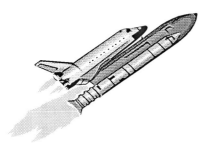

> **Learning is the process of intelligence utilizing a moveable vehicle in order to explore its environment.**

Six weeks after birth marks a difficult time of separation for mothers and infants. Medical doctors and insurance companies suggest a mother is ready to return to the work force at this time. Ideally, a mother should be the constant caregiver for the first three years of her child's life. In our modern times, that is rarely possible. This is a good example of the kind of conflict our adult Inner Selves must learn how to resolve. The mother's *'Unihipili* instinctively feels that she should stay home and care for her infant, but her *'Uhane* knows that in order for the family to survive she must return to work. How well the mother deals with this problem is a reflection of how well she has learned to deal with other conflicts within the Selves. Early separation is also traumatic for the infant. Remember the infant believes that his mother's *'Uhane* is his own. Forced separation of the Selves is the worst experience any human can experience. This separation of mother and infant can be eased somewhat if a caretaker is found who will love and respond to the infant's needs as if she were his own mother.

The period from six weeks to twelve weeks marks an exciting change in the infant Selves. From this point on accelerated rates of learning and accomplishments becomes evident. Once the *'Unihipili* and *'Uhane* begin to work together to control and use the physical body, miracles happen. It is an incredible feat of mastery for the infant Selves to accomplish within a few short months of life!

# *HUNA* TECHNIQUES FOR MASTERING SIX WEEK OLD SKILLS

| **The ability to conceptualize.** |
| --- |

This skill requires the *'Uhane* to be able to extract the separate parts of an action or the specific behaviors and replicate them using the physical body, the emotions, and the mind. Conceptualizing begins with observation. It is much easier for an older child or adult to learn something new by having someone else show them how to do it. The *'Uhane* watches the other person in action, conceptualizes the steps, and then performs the actions. This is the same process an infant uses. This skill is critical to learn for it is this ability that the *'Uhane* uses to conceptualize the end result or the answer to a prayer.

To learn this important skill you need to practice. The *'Uhane* already knows how to do it, but may not have had enough practice. Good nurturers provide opportunities for learning. Choose something new to learn that you know nothing about. Perhaps it is learning how to use a computer, or paint with watercolors, or repair an engine, or play golf. Give yourself the opportunity to learn this new skill by attending a class, hiring someone to teach you, or learning from a relative. Begin by simply observing, watch all the planning, action, and techniques to accomplish the new learning. Go home and conceptualize in your mind, the exact techniques and steps to perform the action. Then experiment and repeat until you have mastered the new learning. Use this same process of observing, conceptualizing, experimenting and repeating, with all your new learnings.

| |
| --- |
| **The Four Steps to Learning:**<br><br>**Observing**<br><br>    **Conceptualizing**<br><br>        **Experimenting**<br><br>           **Repeating** |

## The ability to respond to new stimuli.

It is critical that we be able to respond to new stimuli. This process keeps our developmental skills improving. It doesn't matter what the stimulus is, as long as it is new to us. If you are a sports fan, attend a classical concert. If you prefer to go to the theater, attend a sports event. If you like jazz music, listen to some Country Western. If you are a "couch potato," take up Tai Chi. In other words, choose something exactly opposite to what you normally do. This activates your neuro-circuits in new and different ways. It keeps your 'Uhane and 'Unihipili flexible and able to respond to new situations creatively and productively. You have to practice to keep the Selves open and flexible.

## The ability to separate.

If you have dependency issues, anxiety, emotions or thoughts centering around separation, you may need to master this important skill.

**Acknowledgement.** Acknowledge out loud that you are afraid of being alone, afraid that no one will be around to help you. Discuss these feelings and thoughts with your Inner Selves and write them all down. Let the tears flow as you feel the sadness of separation.

**Forgiveness.** Do a forgiveness ceremony. Ask your 'Unihipili to forgive you for leaving you alone and not listening to your requests for help. Forgive your mother for leaving you when you were so little. Forgive all the other people for leaving you sad and lonely. Forgive yourself for leaving people in your life. Then ask their forgiveness. On a long piece of paper make a list of all the people you have left, physically, emotionally, or emotionally. Call them up or write to them and ask their forgiveness in person. If you don't know where they are, ask your 'Aumakua to find their 'Aumakua and ask for forgiveness.

**Reconstruction.** Do a reconstruction meditation. Imagine you are a six week old baby crying in your bed. See your ideal mother hear your cries and pick you up in her loving arms. Listen to her reassuring voice as she tells you she will never leave you and feel her arms holding you tight. Know that she is telling you the truth. Know that she is always there for you. Look into the eyes of your Holy Mother and realize this truth. We are all connected. All of life is connected. There is no way you can ever be separated from life, separated from Spirit. Know that you can return to this place of perfect connection and perfect peace anytime you want. Give thanks to your 'Aumakua for always being there for you. Give thanks to your 'Uhane for always being there.  Give thanks to your *'Unihipili* for always being there.  Your Three Selves are never alone, but always connected to each other and to the Universal Spirit that permeates all life.

**Ritual.**  Celebrate your connection with Life. On small pieces of paper, write the names of all the people in your life with which you have a connection. Take a ball of colorful yarn and string the yarn around the room from one corner to another.  Affix each name to the strings and remember your connection with that person.  Put your name on at the end.  Leave the yarn in place for a few days remembering how connected you are.  Rewrap your yarn with all the names still attached and put it in a small bag together with 3 natural elements of nature. These elements are a symbol of your connection with the earth.   Place this bag on your personal altar as a symbol of your connection to all of Life through Spirit.

# THE INNER SELVES
# AT TWO MONTHS

At the age of eight weeks or two months the infant Selves will stay awake longer. They will be alert for 15-20 minutes per hour. As the child grows older, he will need less and less sleep. The infant *'Uhane* should be sleeping through most of the night and taking two naps during the day. The *'Unihipili* never sleeps but is always on constant duty taking care of the functions of the body.

The infant Selves will recognize other family members and respond to them by smiling. Physically they will be able to hold the head up and have more control over it. The position of the arms and legs will still be controlled by the position of the head. The *'Unihipili* is now able to change the focus of the eyes and will begin to look and stare at the hands. This staring activity is the first step in the evolution of curiosity. Dr. White says that this staring activity signals that "true interest in, adaptation to, and mastery of the environment has begun." This staring activity will continue until age three. It allows the *'Unihipili* time to give sensory input to the *'Uhane* and allows time for the *'Uhane* to conceptualize the object or movement.

---

### Developmental Skills at Two Months

1. **The ability to be curious. (*'Unihipili* skill)**

2. **The ability to conceptualize movement. (*'Uhane* skill)**

3. **The ability to interact with the environment. (*'Uhane* and *'Unihipili* skills)**

---

Some time soon the Selves will be able to consciously bring the hand to the mouth for sucking. The simple act of consciously moving the hand from one position to another is quite an amazing feat. It requires the full concentration of the *'Uhane* in conceptualizing and directing the movement and the full cooperation of the *'Unihipili* in moving the actual muscles, bones and skin. This is a good description of coordination. Moving the hand to the mouth is the first step in coordination of the two minds. The more often the infant Selves perform this simple movement, the better they can do it and will soon learn to bat at objects.

Batting at objects is the second step in developing the motor skills. When this happens, the Selves will no longer be interested in just observing, but will want to use this new skill of batting to explore. The coordinated motor skill is far more interesting and challenging. Parents have an educational opportunity to bring the world closer to the infant Selves for investigation. Anything that interests a child is educational for the Selves, especially everyday objects used in the daily life of the family.

Two month old infants are exciting to watch. They respond with smiles and want to interact with their environment and with the people around them. They are eager to explore the world.

# *HUNA* TECHNIQUES FOR MASTERING TWO MONTH OLD SKILLS

 **The ability to be curious.**

Curiosity is necessary to learning. The *'Unihipili* is like a sponge, interested in learning, seeing, touching, hearing, tasting, smelling, and feeling everything. As adults we often stifle our curiosity because we don't have time to explore. We're too busy doing all those other things we believe so necessary to life. A good way to master or reclaim this skill of curiosity is provide regular opportunities for the *'Unihipili* to be curious and explore. Some suggestions for reclaiming curiosity are: take a walk in nature and explore anything that catches the attention of the *'Unihipili*; or go to the library and browse through the book shelves, scanning any book that interests the *'Unihipili*; or go shopping and explore stores you wouldn't generally go in. In other words, let your curiosity take you to new areas of exploration. Don't plan to do anything just let follow the interest of your *'Unihipili*. You must give yourself the opportunity to be curious.

 **The ability to conceptualize movement.**

This is an extension of the four week old skill. Each new skill is built on the previous ones. If you feel awkward running or dancing, or doing some other kind of movement, you may need to master this skill. First find someone who is skillful in doing the movement. Spend time observing and then conceptualize the various parts of the movement. Imagine what you would look like if you were to do the movement. Then experiment and repeat the movement until you have mastered it. This is the same method athletes use to improve their skills.

 **The ability to bat at or interact with the environment.**

Batting is the first conscious movement with the environment. If you did not master the skill of batting, you may have experienced tactile deprivation. This can cause shyness or fear of reaching out to touch something or someone. Give your *'Unihipili* permission to explore the

76

world by touch. Feel all the different kinds of textures around you. Run your hands over various surfaces identifying the textures out loud. If the *'Uhane* does not identify the texture correctly, stop and examine it more closely and then the two Selves decide on the word that best describes the texture. Reach out and touch everything in your home. Reach out and touch objects in nature. Spend an afternoon playing in the mud, squishing it between your toes and making mud pies. Go to the beach and spend a day playing in the sand making sand castles and walking along the tide line. Becoming familiar with textures and reaching out to touch them will give you mastery over this skill.

# THE INNER SELVES AT THREE AND FOUR MONTHS

The Inner Selves have come a long way in twelve short weeks. At three months the infant Selves can move the arms and legs independently from the head. They can move the head consciously from side to side while on the back. The *'Uhane* is able to direct the head to turn towards a sound. The *'Uhane* is becoming more aware of the link between hearing and looking. The *'Unihipili* can turn both eyes in at an approaching target and can scan from point to point with skill and speed. The Selves are now interested in tracking objects with this new ability to focus the eyes. The eyes have reached near mature visual capacities. The Selves are now interested in irregularly shaped and multicolored objects. This is the beginning of the appreciation of orderliness and beauty.

With the increased visual capacity, the Selves can look more closely at the hands and fingers. The hands are now unclenched and the fingers become more interesting. Both hands can be brought to the chest where they begin to explore each other. In this exploration the Selves learn much about the abilities of the fingers and hands. The *'Uhane* is gaining more control over directing physical action. The *'Unihipili* is further developing its curiosity. Infants will generally begin to reach for things at this age. This is the next big step in development.

Physically the infant has more muscle strength. The body appears rounder and more sturdy. The *'Unihipili* can begin tactile exploration with the mouth. All infants use the mouth as a tool for exploration until the fingers become the predominant tools. Even as adults we still use our fingers to explore. (Try going shopping without touching anything.)

The three month old infant Selves are still cooing, but now they begin to listen to their own sounds. They become more interested in the sounds going on around them. The emotions of the *'Unihipili* are more balanced because the *'Uhane* is gaining some control over reactions to stimuli. The *'Unihipili* is also able to express some feelings through making sounds. The *'Uhane* is able to categorize the input from the *'Unihipili* and interpret some simple memories.

The three month Selves are fun to be around.  They smile and coo in response to family members.  They can track movement with the eyes and will follow any activity with great interest.  The staring activity continues and the infant needs a variety of opportunities for active observation.

---

### Developmental Skills at Three and Four Months

1. The ability to appreciate beauty and order.  (*'Uhane* skill)

2. The ability to balance the emotions.  (*'Uhane* and *'Unihipili* skills)

3. The ability to interpret sensory input for memory storage.  (*'Uhane* skill)

4. The ability to reach for an object.  (*'Unihipili* skill)

---

The four month old Selves are more exciting, endearing, and lovable with each passing day.  They are easy to respond to and care for.  They continue to refine the skills they have already learned and you can actually see their progress.  The Selves are stronger and can begin to sit up with assistance or when propped with blankets or pillows.  They are now able to move the torso of the body from one side to the other in preparation for turning the body over.  Being able to turn the body over is the first step in learning how to crawl.  When the infant can turn the body back and forth, it is time to place him on the floor for this is the next arena of exploration.

The Selves discover the feet at this age and start chewing on the toes.  The feet were not in view of the eyes until this age and both Selves will be fascinated with them.  The Selves will also start exploring other parts of the body as the arms, hands and fingers become more flexible.  They are exploring the perimeters of their physical body.

**The toes become an exciting new concept to explore.**

79

The Selves will reach for things in earnest now. **The mastery of reaching and grasping is the basis for all subsequent skill learning.** The mastery of this skill indicates the *'Uhane* can conceptualize reaching out with the arm, opening and closing the fingers, and grasping the object while exerting muscle pressure. Through this conceptualization the *'Uhane* directs the *'Unihipili* to move the arm, hand and fingers to perform the action. The Selves need plenty of opportunities to practice reaching for objects that interest them. This marks the beginning of the ability of the infant Selves to bring the world to them. From this point on, they will explore on their own. The next few months are spent in refining the reaching and grasping skill.

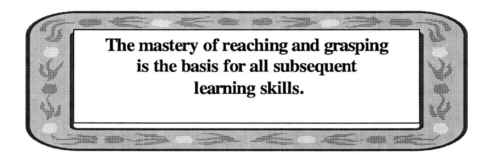

**The mastery of reaching and grasping is the basis for all subsequent learning skills.**

# *HUNA* TECHNIQUES FOR MASTERING THREE AND FOUR MONTH OLD SKILLS

 The ability to appreciate beauty and order.

This skill begins with the ability of the eyes to focus, scan and track objects. It also includes the interest in multicolored irregularly shaped objects. As the eyes focus and scan they register the orderliness of the visual world. This develops into an appreciation for beauty. We all have mastered this skill to some degree evidenced by the beauty of the things we keep around us, our clothes, furniture, cars, yards. The most beautiful and interesting object to all humans is the human form. We begin by focusing on the human eyes and then learn to scan the full body. Beauty doesn't necessarily mean "pretty." There are many beautiful, but not pretty, objects in the world. In some deeper sense we long to feel a part of the beauty around us. If you have some emotions or thoughts centering on not being able to appreciate beauty, you may need to master or reclaim this skill. The first step in appreciation of beauty is to appreciate your own human body, no matter what shape it is in. Study your naked body and reassure your *'Unihipili* that it is beautiful until you feel beautiful. Go to a "glamour studio" and have a professional photograph taken. Every man and woman should have a glamour photograph. Hang your glamour photo in a prominent place in your home.

> **The most beautiful object in the world is the human form.**

Next, go to art shows and spend time focusing on and scanning each piece of art. See beauty from another person's perspective. Have your *'Uhane* pick your "best of show" and then have the *'Unihipili* pick its "best of show" and compare the beauty of each piece. Check out art books from the library and study the works of the Great Masters. Rearrange the furniture and decorations in your home and office for a different perspective of beauty. Keep fresh flowers around you to remind you of the beauty of nature. Spend time outside just sitting in the beauty of nature. It takes time to appreciate beauty and order. Beauty and order bring balance into our lives.

 The ability to balance the emotions.

The foundation of the skill to balance the emotions with logic is built at this age. Expressing emotions through sound begins this process. Listening to the sound of your own voice aids in identifying the emotions your *'Unihipili* is trying to express. If you have emotions or thoughts centered around always keeping your feelings inside and never expressing them, you may need to master this skill. Acknowledge out loud that you are not able to express your feelings and ask your *'Unihipili* to forgive you for stifling this necessary communication.

Ask your *'Unihipili* to cooperate with you as you recreate the foundation for balancing emotions with sound. Babies begin by cooing and gurgling and this is where you begin. Tape your sounds and play them back later. Start by making cooing sounds in the back of your throat. This is where speech and expression develop. Explore all the different pitches, tones and sounds you can create. Tape your sounds when you are feeling emotional. Don't form words with your sounds. After you have explored basic sounds, move on to spontaneous chanting. Chanting is a great balancing technique. It brings you closer to the sounds of the Universe and soothes your inner Self.

**The ability to interpret and categorize sensory input for memory storage.**

This important skill of the *'Uhane* begins at age three to four months. The *'Uhane* reviews the sensory input from the *'Unihipili* and begins to interpret, categorize and send it to the *'Unihipili* for storage in the memory banks. Memories are not stored in the brain, but in the cells of the body. This is the reason memories are brought up if a certain part of the body is stimulated. When the *'Uhane* has not interpreted and categorized the input correctly, the memory is not stored in its proper place. For example, the *'Uhane* of a child whose parents have divorced will often store those memories in the area of "terrible things that happen because it was my fault." The *'Uhane* does not have the correct information at the time to interpret these memories properly. If you have emotions or thoughts centered around memories improperly stored, i.e. "your fault," you may need to master this skill and bring these memories up to date.

**Acknowledge** out loud that you have stored some memories improperly. Ask forgiveness from your *'Unihipili* for not knowing how to interpret the early input and categorize the memories correctly. Next ask your *'Unihipili* to remember these events and bring them to your attention. Write down all the facts and feelings around the memory. Your clue will be if the memories have negative emotions with them. Look at the written memories as an outside observer. Recategorize them and interpret them according to your wiser, older *'Uhane.*

**Reconstruct** the situation again with the new understanding. Reassure your *'Unihipili* that the situation was not its fault. Gather some extra *mana* by breathing deeply several times and instruct the *'Unihipili* to store the correct interpretation and energy with the old memories. Write this new memory and the correct interpretation in your journal.

## The ability to reach out for an object.

This skill is the basis for all subsequent learning. Grasping objects with the fingers is a skill that we all use. Almost every physical action a human performs includes this remarkable skill. An early definition of a human being included the ability to grasp with the thumb. This skill takes both the conceptualization of the *'Uhane* and the actualization of the *'Unihipili* to accomplish. If you have emotions or thoughts centered around your feelings of inadequacy about learning, you may have to master this skill. Most of us have mastered the reaching and grasping with the arm and hand, but we can expand this skill by learning to reach and grasp with our toes. This technique expands the ability of both Selves to refine reaching and grasping by creating new neuro-circuits and motor skills. Place several large objects on the floor and begin by observing the shapes of the each object to be picked up. Conceptualize the movements required to reach out with the leg and foot and grasp them with your toes. Now pick them up. Experiment and repeat the actions until you have mastered picking up the object. Next learn how to write with your toes. Start with individual letters and then progress to words. Remember to observe, conceptualize and then actualize the movement. Have fun learning the process of reaching out and grasping.

# THE INNER SELVES
# AT SIX MONTHS

At six months the infant Selves will be able to roll the body over and sit unaided. Some infant Selves have even begun to move the body around using some form of locomotion. They need to spend a great deal of time on the floor. Only from this position can they learn how to move independently. The drive toward moving the body without help is tremendous. Infants often begin this process by rolling over and over. Others push themselves backwards, while some inch along on their stomachs. Still others bounce along while sitting upright. Whatever the method the infant Selves develop to get the body moving, they eventually end up crawling on hands and knees.

There is an important link between the crossover movement of hands and knees in crawling and the ability of the neuro-circuits to send messages between the hemispheres of the brain. The *'Uhane* must experience this vital crawling activity in order to build these circuits properly. Erik Erikson sees muscle development in terms of "holding on" and "letting go." Everything an infant learns to do, he believes, such as crawl, walk, run, and play are all combinations of these two concepts. In learning how to "hold on" and "let go" the *'Uhane* develops its Will power and the ability to encourage and direct the *'Unihipili*.

```
┌─────────────────────────────────────────────────────────────┐
│              Developmental Skills at Six Months               │
│                                                               │
│   1.  The ability to coordinate and independently move the body. │
│       ( 'Unihipili skill)                                     │
│                                                               │
│   2.  The ability to hold on and let go – the development of the Will.  ( │
│       'Uhane skill)                                           │
│                                                               │
│   3.  The ability to take care of oneself during physical or emotional │
│       illness.  ( 'Uhane and 'Unihipili skills)              │
│                                                               │
└─────────────────────────────────────────────────────────────┘
```

The subject of playpens for an infant is a controversial subject among child development specialists.  A playpen can be a safe place to put an infant, but should not be used regularly.  It becomes a cage for the growing 'Uhane and 'Unihipili, who are anxious to explore the world of their home environment.  The frustration created by caging conflicts with the natural desire to explore.  It is only through exploration that the Selves learn.  We see the effects of caging on zoo animals and in-door pets, which develop all kinds of physical ailments in response to such frustration.  We see the effects of caging adults in tiny apartments and small cubicles in enclosed work spaces as  contributing factors to higher stress levels and other physical and mental ailments.

The Selves have now learned to reach and grasp an object and to release it as well.  Dropping things on the floor from high chairs becomes a wonderful pass time.  The Selves learn cause and effect from these activities.  Reaching, grasping, studying, releasing, dropping, and listening to the noise as an object falls are all elements of cause and effect.  The infant Selves will also bang objects against different surfaces to learn more about their qualities.  Are they soft, hard, bendable, strong, pliable, etc.?  As the visual discrimination progresses, smaller objects become more interesting to the Selves.

The six month old is also learning about social behavior.  The infant wants to be a part of whatever is going on in the family.  The 'Uhane will be awake at least half of the day by this time.  A regular schedule of eating, playing (learning), and sleeping is important for a developing child.  In

> **Rhythm brings energy, comfort and security into our lives.**

fact, a regular schedule is best for all 'Uhane and 'Unihipili.  The rhythm of living is an important factor in experiencing this world.  We gain energy, comfort and security from a rhythmic life.

One day the infant Selves will surprise you by giggling. They will respond all of a sudden to tickling. This is an auspicious occasion for the Selves, for it represents a new concept of "otherness." Since we cannot tickle ourselves, there must be something <u>outside</u> us that tickles. The *'Uhane* has just realized that it is separate from the mother and begins the process of taking its rightful place in the life of the child.

The next physical challenge for the *'Unihipili* is cutting teeth. Some infants get teeth at an early age, while others wait until after they are a year old. Teeth come in when the physical body is ready for them. Cutting teeth is not a comfortable experience. The *'Unihipili* becomes very irritable and cranky. The *'Uhane* cannot help to control the mood when the physical discomfort and emotional response overwhelm the *'Unihipili*, but it tries. Fortunately, the infant's memory is not well developed and he forgets the misery of teething as soon as the tooth emerges.

The six month old Selves are progressing towards independent locomotion. They gain a new perspective of the world from floor level. They can grasp and release objects. The *'Uhane* learns it is separate from the *'Uhane* of the mother. The *'Unihipili* learns the connection between discomfort in the physical body and the control of the emotions and begins to be able to comfort itself with help from the *'Uhane*.

# *HUNA* TECHNIQUES FOR MASTERING SIX MONTH SKILLS

 **The ability to coordinate and independently move the body.**

If you have emotions or thoughts centered around coordination or difficulties in learning, you may need to master this skill. The physical crossover movements of crawling activate the neuro-circuits between the hemispheres of the brain. If you have not reinforced these circuits with an adequate amount of crawling movements, you can master this skill by repeating those movements. You don't have to get down on your hands and knees unless you want to do the exercise in that position. Stand upright, alternate raising the left knee and touching the right hand to the nose with raising the right knee and touching the nose with the left hand. Let the head move naturally in rhythm with the arms. Let the arms swing in exaggerated arcs. Do this alternating movement 50 times morning and night for 7 days, visualizing the neuro-circuits crossing over between the hemispheres of the brain. Rest for 3 days and then repeat for 7 more days. Do the exercise as often as you desire or when prompted by your *'Unihipili*, especially when you are feeling clumsy or uncoordinated or you need to bring yourself back into balance.

Part of learning this skill to move the body independently is to move out of feeling caged. If you work in an office, take breaks and go outside. Eat your lunch outside or at least take a walk at lunchtime. Go to a park or other natural setting. In leisure time, spend a great deal of time outdoors. Nature is our real home, not the cubicles we live and work in. The *'Unihipili* needs to connect with its natural world.

 **The ability to "hold on" and "let go."**

This skill is the basis for exploration and for becoming independent. It is the beginning of the ability of the *'Uhane* to use its Will power. We hold on, observe, conceptualize, let go, and actualize as we move from place to place and from one level to the next. If you have emotions or thoughts centered around holding on and/or the ability to let go, you may need to master this skill. Acknowledge out loud that you have trouble holding on and letting go. Ask your *'Unihipili* to forgive you for not knowing when to let go or hold on. Reconstruct any incidents in which you either held on too long or didn't let go at the appropriate time. Visualize yourself being able to easily let go.  Visualize yourself holding on until the appropriate moment to release.  Write in your journal that you are now able to hold and let go at the proper times.

The ritual for this skill is to mentally, emotionally and spiritually let go of material possessions.  In order for us to move independently, we must not be burdened with so many things.  Go through all of your belongings and give away (release) those objects you have been holding on to, don't use, or don't need.  <u>The key here is to give these items away, not to sell them.</u>  Clean out drawers, closets, kitchens, bathrooms, garages, and storage units.  You are releasing the past in order for your future good to come into your present.  You are clearing out your physical and spiritual space.  The next step is to emotionally release all your treasures.  Visualize life without the treasure until it feels okay and you can release it.  You don't have to actually give the object away or destroy it, but to simply release the emotional attachments.  Next release the people in your life you are emotionally attached to, one by one.  This doesn't mean you don't stop loving them, but that you release them to their highest good.

> **The ability to take care of oneself during physical or emotional illness.**

This skill is an important skill to master because it puts your priorities in order.  When a *'Unihipili* is experiencing distress, anxiety, or illness, the *'Uhane* is responsible to take care of it.  In our modern society, this usually means we pop a few pills and carry on with our same patterns.  We don't stop and listen to what is bothering our *'Unihipili* and take action to correct it.  All of these messages are cries from our *'Unihipili* and must be answered immediately.  Perhaps the body needs a rest in order for the *'Unihipili* to heal it; or the emotions need a time for healing; or the mind needs a diversion.  Whatever the problem, a solution must be found.  The *'Uhane's* first priority is always the needs of the *'Unihipili*.  Acknowledge out loud that you do not always take care of your *'Unihipili* first.  Ask for forgiveness from the *'Unihipili* for not listening and taking action and for putting other things before its needs.  Write a note to your *'Unihipili* stating you will always put its needs first and that you love it.  Post this sign on your bathroom mirror where you can read it every morning and every night.  This is a reaffirmation to your *'Unihipili* that you will remember your priorities.  The ritual for this skill is do something that your *'Unihipili* has wanted to do for a long time.  Call and make arrangements for whatever it is at your first opportunity.   Then plan to spend at least two hours every week doing things your *'Unihipili* wants to do.  Write down this time in your planner or on your calendar and **follow through.**  Don't schedule anything else during that time and don't change the schedule unless you are positive it is okay with your *'Unihipili*.  Your first priority is always your *'Unihipili* and you reaffirm this by action.

# THE INNER SELVES
# AT EIGHT MONTHS

This is one of the most critical times for learning in the life of a human being. At eight months a human becomes a true explorer for he can now move out into the world on his own. John Bradshaw describes the world of the eight month old as a "sensory cornucopia" filled with all kinds of interesting things to explore. The infant Selves are shifting their focus from their own motor skills to interaction with the environment. They want to see everything, touch everything, mouth everything. Erik Erikson says this is the "incorporation state" where the child takes everything in and incorporates it into his life.

Piaget believed that as the infant explores cause and effect, movement patterns of objects, textures, shapes and forms, he acquires the foundation for higher mental abilities. The *'Uhane* is learning the basic substructure of the world. Nothing is more central to higher levels of intelligence than the "substructure of sensorimotor explorations," explains Piaget. This substructure is built by the thousands of simple explorations of small objects the infant performs **without the input of others**.

> ## We learn best without the input of others.

---

### Developmental Skills at Eight Months

1. The ability to recognize cause and effect. (*'Uhane* skill)
2. The ability to communicate ideas and feelings. (*'Uhane* and *'Unihipili* skills)
3. The ability to use others as resources. (*'Unihipili* skill)
4. The ability to use self-discipline. (*'Uhane* skill)

---

The infant Selves should be provided with all kinds of small safe objects to explore. They will practice, practice, and practice with these objects. Predictable sequences are learned through repetition. The objects will be mouthed, banged, struck, thrown, rubbed, sat on, picked up, put down, rolled, stacked, emptied and filled with all sorts of smaller objects. The Selves are especially fascinated with collections of small items with irregular shapes and fine detail.

The skills learned with small objects gives the *'Uhane* the basics of problem solving strategies he can use in other situations. The capacity to perceive oneself as a causal agent and be able to predict the outcome of one's actions is essential to all subsequent experiences of mastery. The *'Uhane* is beginning to conceptualize the body as an outside force by directing the experimental actions of the *'Unihipili*.

The Selves will continue to master the use of the body with improved crawling and now standing alone while hanging on to something. They may even begin to cruise around the furniture. There is

> **We have an inherent desire to ascend the heights.**

an inherent desire in the human being to always ascend to the highest point. The Selves become fascinated with stairs and ascending the heights. Anything that even looks like stairs will be climbed.

The perception and investigation of the environment builds concepts, even stair climbing. The *'Uhane* builds concepts at an incredible rate, once the body is locomotive. Peter Russell states in his book, *Waking Up In Time,* "The more a child learns how to control the world, the more fascinated he becomes with his discoveries—with what he can do and with what he can achieve." The *'Uhane* and *'Unihipili* have learned that they can accomplish more by working together and the more they work together the more they accomplish.

Crying is now used by the two Selves to capture the attention or the company of an adult. Crying is also used to convey frustration or boredom. The different subtle ways to use crying as a way of communicating other needs, besides physical needs, is also a sign that the two Selves have learned to work together.

From eight to ten months an infant will be able to recognize his own name. He will also look at family members when they are named. He will be able to retrieve an object when it is named. He may respond to requests to wave his hand "bye-bye." He may be able to say "mama" or "dada." He is beginning to realize that words are labels for things. The 'Uhane still cannot communicate through speech. Communicating with words not only involves the mastery of the physical mechanics of speech, but also the mastery of the concept of ideas. The infant Selves have been communicating with nonverbal language. Crying and laughing are two ways the 'Unihipili communicates feelings. The 'Uhane is preparing to communicate about ideas. There comes a time just before actual speaking when the Selves will be frustrated because of this inability to make the connection between the idea and the ability to form words. The two Selves desperately want to share feelings and thoughts.

Parents can assist this early communication process. They can teach the infant Selves to use sign language! In landmark research on early communication, authors and child development specialists, Linda Acerdolo and Susan Goodwyn found that babies ages months seven to nine months could communicate directly by using signs. They state in their book, *Baby Signs*, that "It doesn't matter how big or little you are, successful communication with other people makes life better."

## All language is symbolic.

Words are sophisticated symbols for objects or ideas. Since basic language is symbolic, a gesture works just as well. Another word for gesture is sign. Goodwyn and Acerdolo observed that infants **were already signing**, but few parents were paying attention. For example, when an infant holds his arms up in the air, he is making a sign that means "I want you to pick me up." Waving "bye-bye" is another common baby sign. They built on this natural ability and taught infants other simple signs. The frustration level in these signing babies dropped dramatically. They even taught signs to express emotions and the babies were delighted. The Selves cannot express abstract ideas through signing, since the 'Uhane has not yet learned abstract thought. Acerdolo and Goodwyn proved that learning to sign speeded up the process of learning to talk by improving the conceptual skill of the 'Uhane. Infants who signed and then learned to talk moved into the world of words with much less frustration.

Penelope Leach, another early communication specialist, in her book, *Babyhood*, states that we need to "get rid of the common notion that language means talking." She explains that a strong mother/infant bond assures good nonverbal communication between the mother and infant. The mother is sensitive to the tone, volume, sound and mood of her baby's cry or coo. The baby knows his mother's voice and the nuances of her emotions. They have developed a simple mutual system of communication that can be further enhanced by signing. Learning to sign is natural for babies.

The short term memory of the *'Unihipili* begins to develop at this time bringing with it an anxiety about the mother. The eight month old Selves want to know at all times exactly where mother is located. As the Selves explore, they go out into the world and then return to the safe harbor of mother. This separating and coming back together (holding on and letting go) is crucial to the emotional stability and security of the *'Unihipili*. In addition, the *'Unihipili* wants to know where his mother is in case he needs assistance. For the next 12 months the *'Unihipili* will use his mother as both an anchor and an assistant. It will appear as if his world revolves around his mother. He will become shy and anxious around strangers and prefer the arms of his own mother. During this time of exploration, he needs the warmth, consistency, and stimulation that only his mother can provide. Later he will need the same things from his father.

> **Mother becomes the anchor for the Selves.**

The infant Selves are learning from this new experience with the mother. They watch her actions, use her for assistance with "toys," learn the household rules, and rely on her when they feel threatened. The Selves learn from the mother what they can and cannot do. As they watch the mother as a role model, they will begin to express affection, frustration and anger, usually towards her. By her response, they learn the first set of social skills and attitudes they will use later with other family members and other children. This is the first lesson in acceptable social behavior.

20% of the infant's time will be spent in staring at her mother. The Selves are gaining needed information through this staring activity. They will also learn from staring and interacting with the father. They are learning behavior skills from this observing and interacting process.

Psychologist Edward Tolman explains the importance of the learning at this age. In his "cognitive mapping" theory, he states "much of what is learned in childhood may never be operationalized until adulthood." Whatever the child is interested in

> **Much of what we learn as an infant doesn't become operational until adulthood.**

he is learning about, but may not use the information until he becomes an adult. This is not a time for forced learning. Infants already spend every waking minute in learning. The *'Unihipili* feeds sensory information to the *'Uhane* who organizes and conceptualizes it and returns the information to be stored as memories.

Discipline begins here at eight months. Loving and firm discipline from the parents teaches the important skill of self-discipline. The infant Selves are mature enough now to understand the concept of discipline. Discipline should always be loved based. The message the Selves need to understand is "their needs are important, but no more important than anyone else's needs." The *'Uhane* can begin to control the emotional *'Unihipili*, but it must know what is acceptable behavior. The key word here is **begin**. It takes some time for the *'Uhane* to learn, understand and then utilize the concepts of behavior. Shouting and severe physical discipline do not teach the *'Uhane* what it needs to know. The *'Uhane* can only focus its attention for about 27 seconds on any one thing and that has to be at the center of its attention. Distraction and removal are good ways to begin teaching about discipline at this phase of development.

# NEVER USE SHAME TO DISCIPLINE A CHILD!

Shaming at an early age causes enormous problems for adults. Shaming wedges guilt feelings in the sensitive *'Unihipili* that all other similar memories will be built upon. Adults spend years working through these early shaming experiences. Avoid shame by speaking directly to the behavior and not to the child. No child of God deserves to be shamed.

John Bradshaw in *Homecoming: Reclaiming and Championing Your Inner Child*, states that we need discipline "to be free." We need to experience rules in order to be self-ruled. We need to know what the social structure is and how we are to behave in it. We need discipline to develop healthy Will power. We need discipline to help us set our personal boundaries. The art of discipline is exactly what the *'Uhane* needs to learn in order to help the *'Unihipili* control its emotions. When we realize that as nurturers of our Inner Selves we are really teaching self-discipline then we can begin to help the *'Uhane* learn techniques and methods of discipline.

Consistency is necessary to good discipline. The Selves want to know about the permanence of objects and the consequences of action. Are they always the same, or do they change? We teach discipline and social behavior through consistent practices.

The eight month old Selves are embarking on a wonderful journey of exploration. They will need resources, language, opportunity to learn on their own, and self-discipline on this journey. The Inner Selves are on their way to becoming mobile explorers.

# *HUNA* TECHNIQUES FOR MASTERING EIGHT MONTH SKILLS

> **The ability to recognize cause and effect.**

The physical laws of cause and effect are learned by the Selves as they test the physical properties of objects. Behavior laws of cause and effect are more difficult to grasp, but just as important to learn. The ability to control emotional actions or rein in impulses is an element of emotional intelligence (EQ). If you have emotions or thoughts concerning impulsive behavior, you may need to master this skill. First, acknowledge out loud that you do act impulsively, that you act before you think. Ask your *'Unihipili* to forgive you for not being a better guide and teacher and helping it learn to control the impulsive behavior. Ask forgiveness from your *'Uhane* for not trusting it and allowing it to do its job of making decisions. Make an agreement that from this time forward the *'Unihipili* will communicate its feelings first to the *'Uhane* before taking any action and wait patiently until the *'Uhane* decides what to do. Include in this agreement that the *'Uhane* will pay attention immediately and listen to the messages from the *'Unihipili*. This is a skill that is learned by experimentation and repetition. The Selves should be gentle with one another and strive for cooperation. Impulsive behaviors (causes) create consequences (effects). These consequences must be contemplated in advance of action in order to create positive effects. As the *'Uhane* and *'Unihipili* work together to learn behavioral cause and effect, they strengthen the bond and improve inner communication.

> **The ability to communicate ideas and feelings.**

Each trinity of Selves has its own unique language of inner communication. This consists of symbols, feelings, inspiration, words, and prayers. Some symbols and feelings are universal, as Carl Jung found. Others are special to the life and consciousnesses of each trinity. This skill is the mastery of the inner communication system. The *'Uhane* first listens to the messages from the *'Unihipili* and considers its feelings in all decisions. The *'Uhane* talks out loud to the *'Unihipili* explaining its decisions and thoughts. The *'Unihipili* sends clear and accurate messages to the *'Uhane* explaining its feelings. The *'Unihipili* sends clear and accurate prayers to the *'Aumakua*. The *'Aumakua* sends messages of inspiration, intuition and creativity to the *'Unihipili*, who in turn communicates these messages to the *'Uhane*. The three Selves must work together and communicate clearly with each other. This skill is learned through experimentation and repetition through inner dialogue and cooperation. We all naturally talk to our Selves. We build on this natural ability and become aware which part of us is communicating and which part is listening. Practice makes perfect for this skill.

## The ability to begin to use self-discipline.

This skill begins at eight months and is based on the communication ability of the Inner Selves. Self-discipline is allowing the *'Uhane* to make decisions based on logic and to be in charge. Self-discipline is learned through experimentation and repetition. It requires knowledge of the other two skills of this phase. Through inner communication about cause and effect, internal self-discipline begins. We learn this skill through practice. Be aware of situations that arise during the day when the *'Unihipili* wants to act on impulse. Easy situations to recognize focus on money or food. These are good areas in which to practice delaying gratification and using logic. Perhaps the *'Unihipili* wants to buy something to make it feel better. (There is a new term for this behavior – "retail therapy.") Talk with your *'Unihipili* and explain why it is not a good idea to impulsively buy this item. Suggest a time of waiting or substitute another action that will make the *'Unihipili* feel good. Each situation that arises is an opportunity to practice self-discipline.

# THE INNER SELVES
# AT ONE YEAR

The one year old Selves are poised on the brink of another giant leap in development – from crawling to walking. Some babies have already mastered "cruising" or hanging on to and walking around the furniture. Others have taken their first steps. While still others will wait a few more months to walk. Babies walk when they are ready. Encouragement and support are what babies need at this stage.

Avoid putting the Selves into situations sometimes referred to as "passing time." Dr. Burton White explains that "It is difficult to engage a child in active play when psychologically or physically restrained in a high chair, playpen, or car seat." The Selves get restless when restrained for too long a time. They become irritable and cranky. Their natural urge to explore is frustrated as the 'Unihipili is feeling caged and the 'Uhane is pressing for more input. It is this internal conflict that makes the baby cranky.

One year old Selves love the out-of-doors. This is the next great world for exploring. They like to be outside as much as possible. Their indoor environment is shrinking as they explore every aspect of it. A cranky or bored baby will instantly change moods if taken outdoors. Humans are naturally drawn to the world of nature. This is our true environment. We are fascinated by the sights, sounds, tastes, textures and smells of our natural world. (Adult Selves benefit from being out of doors and should spend time each day breathing in the energy and beauty of nature.)

As each month passes, the baby's interest and capacity for learning grows rapidly. The *'Uhane* and *'Unihipili* become better adept at the sensing, interpreting and storing of knowledge. Every act is intentional to gain input for understanding the properties of the physical world. At this age the baby is about 10% people-oriented. By age two this will increase to 20%. The one year old Selves still engage in staring behavior, assimilating information visually. Sometimes it appears the Selves are just hanging around thinking great thoughts. They are actually cataloging and storing information.

When a baby begins to walk around alone, he adds tasting and swallowing to his list of exploring skills. This is the age when a child can get into unsafe materials. The fact that a substance has a foul smell doesn't deter him from trying to taste it.

---

## Developmental Skills at One Year

1. **The ability to walk independently. (*'Unihipili* skill)**

2. **The ability to use other people as resources. (*'Uhane* skill)**

---

The one year Selves continue to refine their motor and conceptual skills. They learn cause and effect through dropping and throwing objects; swinging hinged objects; opening and closing doors; placing relatively unstable objects into upright positions; knocking down and picking up again; putting objects together and taking them apart; putting objects through openings; pouring materials in and out of containers; activating switches that produce light and sound; spinning wheels; manipulating locking devices; and all kinds of finger manipulations. They also strike objects on different surfaces, look at and feel all of the surfaces of an object, and mouth and chew each object. These activities test the physical properties of the object and are cataloged by the *'Uhane* and stored in the memory of the *'Unihipili*.

Mother is still the central figure in the life of the one year old. The *'Unihipili* may be more clinging when he is fatigued or doesn't feel well. You can't spoil a *'Unihipili* by comforting him during these times. Ear problems develop at this age and should be treated as you would a high fever. Boys in particular have more middle ear infections. Boys who have been breast fed have fewer ear infections.

The one year old Selves knows much about the family. They know their mother's limits, her moods, and whether she is gentle and friendly or not. They also know much about their father and other siblings. The *'Unihipili* may exhibit signs of jealousy, especially in regard to her mother, whom she views as her own. The *'Unihipili* will continue to be shy with strangers and will hide behind her mother if they talk to her.

Walking becomes the focus of physical activity. Walking, climbing, moving around in unusual places all help to develop the large muscles of the body. At the same time the clumsiness of the fingers improves with the manipulating of small objects by the small muscles. The Selves will become fascinated with smaller and smaller bits of things such as dust or lint they find on the floor.

The one year old *'Uhane* will begin to understand and associate some behaviors with words. If you put on your coat, she may wave "bye-bye." She certainly understands her name and the names of her family. A one year old understands a great deal more than we believed in the past. If she has been signing, she will begin to associate the word and the sign for the concept. Her *'Uhane* is taking in the language around her and beginning to conceptualize speech.

Between the ages of one and two, the *'Uhane* will begin to speak words. The larynx moves to a lower position taking the tongue with it. By age two speech becomes possible. Speech is a major step forward in the information processing for the *'Uhane*. It can now learn from the experiences of others. At first, speech will be single clear words. Sometimes the clear words will be connected to a long string or collection of sounds, arranged in sentence-like form complete with proper inflections and emphases. The *'Uhane* is practicing the rhythm and drama of its language in preparation for communication. Speaking involves more than just repeating words. It involves mood, intonation, melody and power. The *'Uhane* will fill in the sentences with words as her vocabulary increases. Language mastery is important for the development of social skills. As the child matures, the *'Uhane* will learn how to use language to express abstractions. The *'Unihipili* is delighted with the prospects of spoken communication for now it can express its feelings more directly.

## The infant Selves imitate adult behavior.

The one year old Selves learn from observation, experimentation and repetition. They are now able to learn by imitating adult behavior. If they observe an adult yelling, they will imitate that behavior. If they see an adult mistreating a pet, they will try to mistreat it in the same way. If they are spanked, they will hit their toys or their siblings. If they see love expressed with hugs they will express love by hugging instead of hitting.

When the Inner Selves begin walking they cross over into the world of adults. They enter mainstream society. In 52 short weeks they have taken an almost helpless physical body and mastered all its elements to be able to use it to move out into the world to explore. They know how to use adults as resources. They are beginning to speak in words to share their ideas and feelings with others.

# *HUNA* TECHNIQUES FOR MASTERING ONE YEAR OLD SKILLS

 The ability to walk.

This important skill is learned from age 12 – 18 months. A child walks when he or she is ready, but can progress faster with encouragement. Walking involves muscle strength and coordination of brain and limbs. It involves balance, vision, hearing, and motivation. It involves a certain amount of cooperation between the *'Uhane* and *'Unihipili*. They have now learned how to conceptualize the act of walking and the actualization of the movement.

The ability to walk is based on the ability of the *'Uhane* to use its developing Will power to let go and try new things. If you are uncertain about trying new things, you may have to master this skill. One of the ways to practice is to learn to swim. Swimming is much like walking. You have to learn how to maneuver in a new medium. If you already know how to swim, learn how to swim better or learn how to dive. In learning to walk or swim, you have to engage your intention (Will) and let go. You learn how to use the physical body in new ways and you have to learn to trust yourself.

 The ability to use other people as resources.

It is good to be independent and self-reliant. However, one of the major ways in which we learn is through imitation and example. Some people have difficulty is asking for help. If you have difficulty in asking for assistance, you may need to master this skill. Practice is the key to learning this skill. Asking for assistance involves trust. You must be able to trust that the person you asked will provide the assistance or answer. Some people are unable to provide assistance and we must learn to seek out those who are best qualified to have the answer. Begin by taking a class. You rely and trust the instructor to assist you to learn the subject. Computer education is a good place to start. You learn computer skills by observation, experimentation (actually using the computer), and repetition. You must trust the tech support person because you cannot possible learn everything about computers. Practice trusting and using other people as resources every day.

# THE INNER SELVES
# AT TWO YEARS

This last phase of development of Infancy is the most dreaded time by parents. It is often referred to as "the terrible twos." It can be described as the most exciting, the most difficult, and the most interesting of all the phases. The Selves develop language, social and intellectual skills, and expand their curiosity. The next comparable phase of development for the Selves occurs in adolescence, when they must break away from parents and family and begin the human cycle all over again.

"Do it myself!" is the motto of the two year old Selves. They will want to do it alone, even though they are not physically capable. The Selves are so excited about using their increased abilities that they don't realize the body has not caught up to the conceptualized activity. Control is the real issue at this age. It is the recognition that the two Selves are separate from the mother. Her *'Uhane* has been a good substitute for the immature *'Uhane* of her child, but now the child's *'Uhane* wants to take its rightful place. His *'Unihipili* has been accustomed to his mother's *'Uhane* making all the decisions and taking care of him. Now, all of a sudden there is another *'Uhane* wanting control and the *'Unihipili* isn't sure if it likes the idea. The *'Unihipili* is fearful about this change in control. So we have a rebellion on two fronts. The child's *'Uhane* rebelling against the control of the mother's *'Uhane* and the *'Unihipili* rebelling against its *'Uhane* taking control.

This control struggle is the basis of all the negativism associated with the two year old Selves. This struggle for control will go on for the next 10 years until the *'Uhane* finally gains the upper hand. However, the *'Uhane* still needs guidance in how to guide and direct the *'Unihipili* and the parents are responsible to teach it. The Inner Selves will eventually learn how to cooperate fully, but it takes time and patience.

---

### Developmental Skills at Two Years

1. **The ability to use fantasy.**  (*'Unihipili* and *'Uhane* skills)

2. **The ability to understand and follow the Basic Commands.** (*'Uhane* skill)

3. **The ability to begin to identify emotions.**  (*'Unihipili* skill)

---

One of the ways in which parents can facilitate this changeover is to let the child make more decisions. The *'Unihipili* will want to jump into the decision process with a feeling response first, but by offering choices to the *'Uhane* the feelings can be processed with the choice.  This is the ideal method of <u>logic</u> being in charge instead of the <u>emotions.</u>  At first these decisions are simple, such as which clothes to wear or what to eat for lunch.  The parents retain control by offering appropriate, but limited choices.   If they allow the child's *'Uhane* to start deciding, everyone is happy.  As a child matures and learns to make good choices, the parents release more control.  At about age 12, a child should be able to control his or her own life.  If parents wait until the child is ready to leave home to teach him to make good choices, he will have lost valuable time and experience.

> **Decision making begins at age two.**

The two year old *'Uhane* began to say some words at about age 18-20 months.   Her *'Unihipili* now has about 300 words stored in its memory and the *'Uhane* can use these words with all the major grammatical forms of the native language.  The *'Uhane* has learned that a word can represent an abstract idea.  For instance, at eight months the word "bottle" meant her bottle.  At two years the word "bottle" can mean any number of different bottles.  The Selves can now express their needs directly to the mother, who continues to hold a central place in the child's life.  The Selves are more interested in other people and their social style is already established.  They will express sensitivity to particular situations as the *'Unihipili* expresses its feelings to the *'Uhane* for translation into words.  The verbal expression of feelings is a sure sign  that the two Selves are beginning to communicate with each other.

> **Words help to express feelings.**

The two year old Selves can get and hold the attention of adults in a more logical way, rather than by just using crying.  They can even direct adults in various activities showing a comprehension of advanced planning.  They are becoming especially good about expressing affection and annoyance.  These are not very subtle expressions, however.

A major step in the development of the human at age two is the growing ability to use fantasy. This is an extremely important ability to encourage. It is especially important later in life. The ability to fantasize and visualize is a critical part of the *Huna* prayer process. The visualization of the perfect answer to the prayer is sent to the *'Aumakua,* who creates the answer according to this visualized pattern. The ability to do this begins here at age two. Fantasy is also used to help develop the ability to put oneself in another's place. This is another element of Emotional Intelligence that begins at two and is fully developed at age eight. This a perfect time to begin teaching the *Huna* way of "no hurt." A child can fantasize about the consequences of his actions and learn that he can do anything he wants, as long as he does not hurt someone else or himself. "No hurt" is really the foundation of all our social and religious laws.

The two Selves are better off when they choose most of their own activities within an environment that relates well to their developmental level. Parents select that environment and provide suitable learning experiences. Adults should not hover over children. Children learn by themselves. Adults cannot force them to learn. In fact, there are several things we cannot force any one else to do: learn, eat, sleep and eliminate. These must all come from a desire within to accomplish the action.

## A CHILD IS AS MUCH HEART AS MIND...

The child at this phase of development is, as Dr. White says, "...a complicated creature who is at least as much heart as he is mind." The *'Unihipili* needs as much love and attention as the *'Uhane.* A good way for parents to deal with the intense emotions that surface during the this phase is to help the child's *'Unihipili* learn to identify the emotion. By naming the emotion and acknowledging it, we gain control over it. This important information is then stored in the memory. Identifying emotions is another element of Emotional Intelligence.

By age two the Selves have embarked on the exploration of using ideas and images and practicing solving problems by using logic. Before this time problems were solved by physical action. Now the *'Uhane* can image the problem in its mind and solve it <u>before</u> directing the action of the *'Unihipili.* Elementary abstract thought has begun. The *'Uhane* cannot count, but can recite the numbers with the help of the *'Unihipili.* It does know that two cookies means one cookie plus another cookie, but not the concept of "two." The Selves are still interested in objects, especially those of everyday life. They still want to know where mother is located and will leave their play often to check.

Do not try to toilet train a two year old. Instead let the child learn by imitation. A child's body, emotions and mind must all be ready before he will be able to control elimination. Some children are ready at age two, but most children are not. The 'Uhane and the 'Unihipili must be able to work together with the idea, the feeling, and then the control, before toilet training can happen. Don't be in a hurry. Many children are traumatized by forced toilet training before their bodies are ready.

> **We must all learn the Basic Commands and how to follow them.**

The two year Selves are able to learn what Jim Fay and Grant Foster, authors of *Parenting With Love and* Logic, call the Basic German Shepherd Commands. These are important basic instructions of **sit**, **stay**, **stop** and **go**. Each child needs to know and be able to follow these instructions. They are used in many types of discipline programs and are the basis of good social behavior.

One of the challenges of the two year old is to learn how to express anger and frustration in appropriate ways. These expressions, better known as tantrums, are the negative behavior most associated with this phase of development. Do not permit the two year old 'Unihipili to get into the habit of throwing tantrums. This takes patience and consistent actions by the parents. Tantrums are either a dramatic response of the child's 'Unihipili to being controlled by his own 'Uhane or a direct conflict between the child's 'Uhane and the 'Uhane of the parents. In either case, the parents must catch the tantrum before it becomes full blown and teach the child how to handle the situation, keeping in mind that the child's 'Uhane must learn control. Do not yell at the Selves or lecture them. Never shame the Selves, but speak to the specific behavior. The best method is to remove them to another location. This gives the 'Unihipili the opportunity to calm down and the 'Uhane the opportunity to make a choice. Consistency and patience are the keys.

The two year old Selves are more complicated for parents to manage. It is well worth the effort to begin proper and consistent and loving discipline at this time. If discipline is not begun in this phase, it will be more difficult in subsequent phases. Two year old Selves are charming, interesting and loving human beings. The struggles they go through to move into Toddlerhood are tremendous and they need all of the love and patience and wisdom their parents can provide.

# *HUNA* TECHNIQUES FOR MASTERING TWO YEAR OLD SKILLS

## The ability to use fantasy.

This skill is one of the most important skills for all humans. We need this ability to see ourselves in the future and to predict the consequences of future actions. At age two the ability to see into the future has not yet developed, but the beginning of the ability to fantasize has. If you have emotions or thoughts about your ability to fantasize, you may need to master this skill. This is a practice skill learned through experimentation and repetition. We all have the ability to fantasize, but some of us may not have practiced as much as others. Fantasy is made of all the learning modes, visual, auditory and tactile. If you have trouble fantasizing, you may be trying to visually fantasize from an auditory mode. To switch to a visual mode, you look up to your right. Actually move your eyes upward to the right. By moving your eyes you are accessing the part of the brain that controls your visual mode. Moving the eyes to the upper left will help access visual constructs. Begin fantasy practice by listening to guided meditations. Even with your eyes closed, move them to the upper right and left as the meditation proceeds as you visualize the instructions. Guided meditations on tape are good tools for learning fantasy. Read fantasy books and picture and feel yourself in the role of the hero or heroine. Day dreaming is a part of the fantasy skill, but be careful where you do it. Some auto accidents happen because the drivers were daydreaming.

## The ability to understand and follow the Basic Commands.

Our social behavior depends on the Basic Commands of sit, stay, stop, and go. *'Unihipili* who are not easily controlled or directed have not yet learned these Basic Commands. Again we have to observe, experiment and repeat. Make a game out of seeing if your *'Unihipili* remembers and can follow these commands. Whenever you think of it, say one of the commands out loud and see if your *'Unihipili* can follow it. Praise your *'Unihipili* for doing a good job. The better he or she learns these basic commands the easier it will be for the *'Uhane* to control and direct more complicated actions.

## The ability to identify emotions.

The basic emotions are easy to identify, but more subtle ones are harder. The ability of the *'Unihipili* to identify the emotion and share this information with the *'Uhane* is an important skill to learn. If you often have difficulties correctly identifying emotions and interpreting them, you many need to master this skill. Again it is a matter of practice. When you find yourself emotionally reacting to a situation, stop and have a discussion with your *'Unihipili*. You might be surprised to discover the emotion you interpreted was not the emotion felt by your *'Unihipili*. Double check your interpretation before making any assumptions. Your *'Unihipili* may not want to share its true emotion because it may feel you have not listened in the past. Reassure your *'Unihipili* that you <u>will listen and wait</u> until you fully understand before making a decision. You can make a guessing game out of this practice. Remember to praise the *'Unihipili* for cooperating and doing such a good job.

# THE DEVELOPMENTAL PHASE OF TODDLERHOOD

## THE INNER SELVES FROM THREE TO FIVE YEARS

This next phase of development is called Toddlerhood. It is a time for fine tuning the discernment of the physical world in preparation for moving into the social world. The development of the two Selves during the first three years of life is linked to the quality of play. This "play" is really accelerated learning through experience. The first three years are spent in exploration and mastery of the physical world. The next three years are spent in using this knowledge to manipulate and construct.

Piaget calls this next phase of development "preoperational thought." The child's brain grows to 2/3 of its full size by age three. At no other time of life will the brain evolve with such complexity and speed. With the accelerated growth of the brain, the child masters language. The acquisition of language aids the child from age three to five to develop tools for representing abstractions internally. Among these tools are imitation, imagery, symbolic play, and symbolic drawing. The toddler's knowledge is tied to his own perceptions of the world.

Creativity blossoms in this phase through fantasy play. Scientists do not understand the meaning or importance of fantasy play. They do know that it is a distinguishing characteristic of well-developed children. Students of *Huna* know that the ability to imagine well is crucial to the prayer process.

Parents have a great opportunity to encourage original thinking in this phase by supporting the thinking ability of the child's *'Uhane*. They can model logical thought by talking out loud about the steps they are taking to solve a problem and how to use substitute objects. As a child's *'Uhane* learns to solve specific problems, he is learning general strategies for solving other problems.

Toddlerhood is a wonderful time. A child's language skills have developed in addition to his conceptualization skills. You can now carry on an intelligent conversation with the three year old. Such a conversation may mystify or stump you, for this is the time of the big WHY questions. The toddler Selves are insatiably curious and that curiosity will be at the forefront of every activity. Curiosity is a prerequisite for higher learning. However, curiosity can lead to unpredictable adventures.

The dominant characteristic of this phase is activity. Toddlers are busy, busy, busy. They are always talking, moving, and planning. They seem to be active from the time they get up until they go to sleep at night. The Selves are driven by curiosity and activity, which help to refine their skills. Imitation is the way that toddler Selves learn in this phase of development. They love to imitate adults and often "play" at grown-up activities.

Fantasy play is imitative. It is a way of gaining self-control. By using fantasy the Selves are freed from real events and can experience different situations and alternative outcomes in non-ordinary reality. They will include a number of activities in the same fantasy. Just as the Selves learned about the physical properties of things, they are now learning about the properties of cause and effect in the social world.

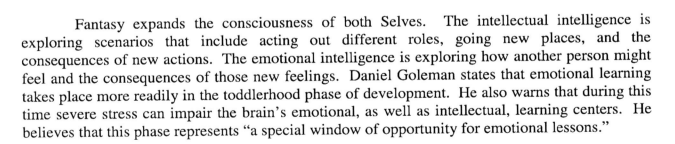

**Fantasy expands the consciousness of the two Selves.**

Fantasy expands the consciousness of both Selves. The intellectual intelligence is exploring scenarios that include acting out different roles, going new places, and the consequences of new actions. The emotional intelligence is exploring how another person might feel and the consequences of those new feelings. Daniel Goleman states that emotional learning takes place more readily in the toddlerhood phase of development. He also warns that during this time severe stress can impair the brain's emotional, as well as intellectual, learning centers. He believes that this phase represents "a special window of opportunity for emotional lessons."

Goleman defines emotion as "a feeling and its distinctive thoughts, psychological and biological states, and range of propensities to act." He names the primary emotions as: anger, sadness, fear, enjoyment, love, surprise, disgust, and shame. People all over the world, no matter the culture or level of civilization, recognize the facial expressions of these universal emotions. He explains that the logic of the emotional mind *('Unihipili)* is associative. It takes "elements that symbolize a reality, or trigger a memory of it, to be the same as that reality." A smile is symbolic of enjoyment. An open mouth is a symbol of surprise. In this world of symbols, anything is possible. In other words, fantasy is the same as reality to the *'Unihipili.* We can see how the development of fantasy in the toddler is the development of the emotional mind of the *'Unihipili.* Toddlerhood is focused on this emotional development.

# The skills for emotional intelligence are:

1. The ability to control emotional impulses.

2. The ability to read another's innermost feelings.

3. The ability to handle relationships smoothly.

# THE INNER SELVES
# AT THREE YEARS

The toddler grows out of the "terrible twos" and into the "thrilling threes." The three year old Selves are a joy to be around. They have learned to manage frustration better, especially if the parents have allowed the *'Uhane* to make choices. The *'Uhane* and *'Unihipili* have learned how to cooperate better, not in every situation, but within reason. They are able to express curiosity with words and can carry on a very good conversation with adults.

The *'Uhane* is now able to conceptualize numbers. This begins with the idea of "1, 2, 3." As the *'Uhane* matures, it will be able to conceptualize larger and larger numbers. Counting everyday items and actions helps the *'Uhane* develop this conceptualization of numbers and to begin to categorize more efficiently. If counting is learned as a game, the *'Unihipili* is willing to participate and creates strong memory patterns for the numbers.

At three, the *'Uhane* is beginning to develop a rudimentary sense of time, which involves some appreciation for the future. He realizes that his needs will eventually be met, if his *'Unihipili* has a little patience. This has helped reduce the frustration level. The ability to handle impulses and wait for gratification is an emotional skill the *'Unihipili* must learn.

The removal of diapers is a big step toward refinement of locomotive skills for the three year old Selves. The legs and body can move in new ways and they can master running, jumping, hopping and even dancing. Three year olds love to dance. A tricycle is a good toy for this age. It not only provides opportunity for muscular development, but also a new vehicle for exploration that can be propelled by the Selves. It connects the toddler to the adult world in a new way.

---

### Developmental Skills at Three Years

1. The ability to handle impulses and delay gratification. (*'Unihipili* skill)

2. The ability to soothe oneself. (*'Uhane* skill)

3. The ability to recognize the emotions of others. (*'Unihipili* and *'Uhane* skills)

4. The ability to create ritual. (*'Unihipili* and *'Uhane* skills)

---

The *'Unihipili* has stored between 400-600 words in its memory. The *'Uhane* has mastered most of the language needed for everyday adult conversation. Language is more powerful and concrete to a child than to an adult. The power of words is essential in a child's fantasy world. He will be able to use language to learn new things. You will hear the *'Uhane* talking out loud to the *'Unihipili* about what is happening in the fantasy. Don't discourage this activity. Adults need to talk out loud to themselves too. It is the best way for our *'Uhane* to communicate with our *'Unihipili*.

> **The spoken word is powerful.**

Talking out loud is a good indicator that the *'Uhane* is learning how to soothe the *'Unihipili*. Being able to soothe oneself is part of emotional intelligence. In fantasy play the child is able to very quickly act out a broad range of situations and the emotions involved. This might include punishment and forgiveness, harm and healing, fear and courage, all within the boundaries of imagination. These are invaluable lessons for real life. Through fantasy, the *'Uhane* learns the consequences of actions and emotions.

The initial emotional responses of the three year old *'Unihipili* are still vigorous, but it is learning how to handle them in more appropriate ways. Parents can support this process by helping the *'Unihipili* identify and name the emotion he is feeling. The *'Unihipili* can learn to identify the emotions other people are feeling and how they respond to the feeling. These are lessons in learning appropriate ways to express feelings. Making this process into a game will make it more interesting to the *'Unihipili* and *'Uhane*.

These lessons about emotions are also learned in group play. The three year old Selves are ready to interact with other children, but only one or two at a time. Building relationships is another aspect of emotional intelligence and the Selves need opportunities to do this. At this age, however, one or two new people are all the Selves can handle.

The *'Unihipili* is still demanding in one aspect of life. The *'Unihipili* has discovered ritual and these rituals must be exactly followed every time. If the rituals are not followed precisely, the *'Unihipili* does not feel right. His sense of security and stability are shaken. These rituals represent the *'Unihipili's* efforts to bring order and meaning to life. An example of this is the bed time ritual for the three year old. We will continue to use rituals for the rest of our lives to celebrate important and sacred moments.

# *HUNA* TECHNIQUES FOR MASTERING THREE YEAR OLD SKILLS

> **The ability to handle impulses and delay gratification.**

These are two elements of Emotional Intelligence we learn at age three. If it is difficult for you to delay gratification and handle impulses, you may need to master these skills. You begin by practicing. Handling impulses is a continuation of the skill you mastered in the two year old phase. Go back and read the techniques in that section. Delaying gratification is really teaching the *'Unihipili* to have patience. The *'Uhane* is the teacher of patience. At three years the Selves begin to have a concept of the future. Delaying gratification is part of that future concept. Gratification makes the *'Unihipili* feel good. The *'Uhane* can start with little things first. Wait an hour before eating cookies. Wait until the weekend to go to the show, rent a video, buy tools. You begin slowly and work up to larger gratification issues, such as waiting to celebrate until after work is completed. In this learning process the *'Uhane* must follow through with the delayed gratification at the promised time. The *'Unihipili* is more likely to cooperate when it trusts the word of the *'Uhane*. This skill is also about building trust between the Selves.

> **The ability to soothe oneself.**

It is the responsibility of the *'Uhane* to soothe the *'Unihipili*. The Selves have been relying on the mother and father for soothing up to this point. Now is the time for the *'Uhane* to take over this important responsibility and shift emotional dependence from the outside to the inside. Part of caring for others is the ability to soothe them. The *'Uhane* shows its love by soothing the *'Unihipili*. This soothing can be expressed in many ways. One way is through the power of the spoken word. Another is listening and acknowledging the feelings of the *'Unihipili*. And another way is to take action to protect and love the younger Self. The *'Unihipili* depends on its older brother or sister to take care of it. You begin to soothe yourself by acknowledging the existence of the *'Unihipili* and learning about its characteristics and needs. The next step is to accept the responsibilities of the *'Uhane* and begin to demonstrate love towards the *'Unihipili*. Love does not mean the emotional Self does whatever it wants to, but is gently guided and taught by the intellectual *'Uhane*.

## The ability to recognize the emotions of others.

This skill is built on the previous skill of learning to identify the emotions of the *'Unihipili*. Through fantasy play the Selves begin to identify the emotions of others. This is an element of Emotional Intelligence. By recognizing the emotions of others, the *'Uhane* can make better choices and anticipate consequences of action. Begin by asking your *'Unihipili* to cooperate and guess how different people are feeling. It helps if you can check with them to confirm your guess. You base your guess on facial expressions, body language, and tone of voice, all of which are important nonverbal clues. Practice when standing in line, waiting in lobbies, or at any other time. The more you practice, the more you can recognize the nonverbal emotional clues.

## The ability to create ritual.

This is a skill that can also be used in the soothing process. All *'Unihipili* love ritual. It comforts them, brings order to their lives, and makes an impression that something important is happening. Ritual is sacred movement and can involve prayers, meditation, music, blessings, and special words. Ritual is important to the lives of the Selves because it raises the moment to the sacred. Three year olds begin this love of ritual with bedtime rituals. If any portion of the ritual is not followed, they feel insecure. Rituals bring us security. As adults our morning and evening rituals bring us security. Habits are a form of ritual. Rituals anchor us in this reality and shift us into nonordinary reality. We use ritual to honor special occasions, such as marriage, birth, and memorials.

Sacred rituals should be a part of our everyday life. They bring the three Selves together in a way no other action can accomplish. They integrate the emotional, mental and spiritual into a perfect wholeness. Rituals bring the *'Aumakua* into your life in a very real way. If you have no rituals in your life, it is time to learn this skill. Rituals are personal acts. Whatever is meaningful to both your *'Uhane* and *'Unihipili* should be included. The sacred aspect of your beliefs should also be included. Begin by constructing a personal altar in your bedroom or living room on which you place meaningful objects. Candles are important ritual objects. Attend ritual services or ceremonies and see which aspects are meaningful to you. Add these to your personal rituals. Perform your rituals on a regular basis and to commemorate special occasions in your life. Rituals are sacred celebrations.

# THE INNER SELVES
# AT FOUR YEARS

The four year old Selves are usually quite precocious. They will be admired in public for being charming, cute and lovable. This admiration is good for the Selves. They should be praised for achievements. Praise builds self-esteem.

By four years of age the 'Unihipili has about 1000 words in his memory. The 'Uhane knows how to use past tense, plurals, and the possessive and conditional forms of words. Where he was able to <u>name objects</u> during the first stage of language acquisition, he will now be able to use words and sentences to <u>describe actions</u>. Don't be discouraged if the four year old is not speaking much. Albert Einstein did not speak until he was four years old explaining that he didn't have anything to say.

The four year old Selves will be able to recite the alphabet from memory, especially if it was learned through song. The 'Uhane will recognize individual letters on signs or in books if they are printed in large capitals. Books are important to the four year old Selves and they should have plenty of new books every week to look at and have read to them. Some libraries will issue library cards to young children to encourage them to read.

## Developmental Skills at Four Years

1. The ability to use abstract objects for learning. ( *'Uhane* skill )

2. The ability to express feelings through art. ( *'Unihipili* skill )

3. The ability to differentiate feelings and actions of oneself and others. ( *'Uhane* and *'Unihipili* skills )

4. The ability to realize and learn about the spiritual world. ( *'Uhane* and *'Unihipili* skills )

The Selves in this phase love to draw and color. Their pictures are bold and colorful, not tiny and detailed. The motor skills of hand and fingers are still developing. The pictures instead have emotional content. Four year old pictures remind me of the paintings created by Koko, the gorilla. Koko was taught to sign and communicate with humans. Koko's pictures represent her emotions about objects, people, other animals, or situations. When you look at Koko's pictures you understand them on an emotional level. The pictures of the four year old Selves are similar. The emotional content is the important aspect of this kind of art.

**Art is a wonderful way to express emotions.**

Play with other children can now be expanded to include more individuals. Four year old Selves are excited to interact with other Selves. However, they still need time to play by themselves in their fantasy world. Regular attendance at play groups, nursery school, or preschool programs are good experiences for the Selves. These should be opportunities for expanding curiosity, rather than for formal education. The Selves at four years are not quite ready to move into the formal educational environment.

The *'Uhane* can now consider alternatives and anticipate the consequences of actions. All those hours spent repeating and experimenting with small objects taught it much about cause and effect. The Selves are learning about cause and effect of actions and behavior through fantasy play. The *'Unihipili* is still mostly self-centered, but is sometimes willing to share. The short term memory is fully developed now and the *'Unihipili* can even point out discrepancies.

The Selves do not yet understand accidental occurrences. They will take on the fault of whatever has happened even it the incident was accidental. Things that happen outside their influence don't make any sense. The Selves also believe that anything that moves is alive. The abstract idea of outside animation hasn't come into their consciousness. Nonordinary playmates may appear at this phase of development. There is such a thin line between fantasy and reality that some characters cross over from one realm to the other.

The expression of feelings is still strong for the four year old 'Unihipili. These feelings should not be ridiculed or brushed aside. They are real feelings and need some form of legitimate expression, otherwise they will get pushed deep down into the 'Unihipili, causing problems in adulthood. Discovering that feelings and actions are two different things is quite an achievement for the four year old Selves. They will comprehend this difference more as they mature. The Selves also begin to take the feelings of others into account before they make decisions. They learn how to do this by the example of the people around them. Talking out loud about what is happening and pointing out specific nonverbal signals of emotions are important tools to teach the Selves.

Independence is a skill that continues to grow during this phase. The four year old Selves can do more things and should be encouraged to do as much as possible for themselves. They will probably want to help out with any task an adult is doing, especially the father. Fathers step into the lives of children in a more important way at age four. Fathers are good teachers and are the role model for the logical mind of the 'Uhane. Fathers naturally foster independence and can include the Selves in their activities. The Selves feel very much a part of the family at this age and should be taught to share some of the work of the family. Sharing energy, time, talents and decisions is an important step in human development. It takes the Selves to a new level of realization of the inclusiveness of all life. Inner Selves, who do not have this opportunity early in their lives, unrealistically rely on other people later in life and suffer great frustration and disappointment. The Selves should be taught to share outside the family through the example of the parents.

> **Fathers step into the lives of the Selves and begin to teach about the logical 'Uhane.**

All kinds and forms of music fascinate the four year old Selves. They delight in rhythm and singing. They will enjoy appropriate live music, especially if parents play musical instruments. Family singing is a wonderful way to create love and memories of closeness and enjoyment. Four year old 'Unihipili can memorize the words and melodies to several of their favorite songs. Both Selves enjoy music and singing.

Abstract thinking has begun in the four year old. The Selves begin to ask questions about God. Simple answers are the best at this age. The world of Spirit appears to be a fantasy world to the young Selves. They instinctively know about God and may express insightful knowledge to adults. Use their own words and concepts to discuss the spiritual dimension. It is as important for a child to learn about the spiritual world as it is to learn about the physical world. Now is the time to begin a good program for spiritual training. They will love to go to Sunday School and church and join other family members in prayers and meal blessings.

Discipline should continue with love and logic. This method is an excellent way to teach both the *'Uhane* and *'Unihipili.* First we empathize with the *'Unihipili* about what has happened. By empathizing first we show love and then we speak to the specific behavior. We allow the *'Uhane* to think and speak about the consequences and how to solve the problem. If appropriate, we offer two choices to the *'Uhane.* If the child's *'Uhane* does not choose, the parents' *'Uhane* step in and choose. The parents control the choices while the *'Uhane* practices choosing. The Selves are never shamed, but always talked to in loving ways. They are loved, but have to learn how to make good choices and behave in acceptable ways. These are two skills they will need in school and as adults.

> # Discipline with love and logic and consistency.

# *HUNA* TECHNIQUES FOR MASTERING FOUR YEAR OLD SKILLS

## The ability to use abstract objects for learning.

One of the indicators of a mature *'Uhane* is the ability to use abstract objects for learning. This skill will be used all during the lives of the Selves. It is a way to gain information. Abstract objects such as books, television, videos, audio tapes, computers, all help the *'Uhane* gain needed information. This is an essential skill in modern society. We are in the Information Age and need this skill to be successful. You learn this skill through practice. If you do not know how to use a computer, take a course or internet class. Decide on any new subject and use books, videos, television courses, or a computer to learn it. Explore your learning resources.

## The ability to express feelings through art.

This skill allows the *'Unihipili* to add another appropriate outlet to the expression of its feelings. This is emotional art and is not intended to be full of details. Psychologists use this kind of Inner Child Art Therapy to help clients connect with emotions they have suppressed for many years. Whether you have suppressed emotions or want to expand the expression ability of the *'Unihipili*, this skill is important to learn. And it is fun to do! You can use oil paints, acrylics, tempera, pastels, chalk, or crayons and large sheets of paper. Finger paint is a good medium for this exercise too. In fact, it is the medium with which most four year old *'Unihipili* begin.

First quiet the mind and center yourself. The object is to keep the *'Uhane* observing and not participating or trying to direct the activity. The *'Uhane* remains a nonjudgmental observer throughout the entire process. The *'Unihipili* makes all the decisions to create this work of art. The *'Unihipili* must create the painting by using the nondominant hand. This helps the *'Uhane* stay out of the process. Whatever comes forth from the *'Unihipili* in creating this art piece is exactly right. Allow the *'Unihipili* to make as many pictures in one sitting as it wants to create. If the *'Unihipili* is feeling particularly emotional, suggest putting that emotion on paper. The *'Uhane* will learn much about the emotional nature of the *'Unihipili* through mastering this skill. Keep all of these pictures and display the latest work on your refrigerator or other prominent place. After the work is completed, discuss the meaning with your *'Unihipili*. Review the works of art often and admire the talent of your *'Unihipili* to creatively express itself.

**The ability to differentiate between feelings and actions.**

This skill improves the cooperation between the Inner Selves. It is the first step in realizing there are two separate minds in the physical body – the emotional mind and the logical mind. As a nurturing parent, it is our responsibility to help both the *'Uhane* and *'Unihipili* learn this skill. We learn how to differentiate by observation and inner dialogue. We observe our own Selves and the Selves of others, watching for emotions and the reactions and actions that follow. It takes practice to be able to discern a reaction from an action. We also observe those adults who have learned to "think before they act" and imitate their behavior.

 **The ability to realize and learn about the spiritual world.**

We all know at a deep level that we are more than physical beings. We call this other part of us the spiritual. Some children at age four remember where they were before they were born. Others are still connected to the spiritual world and can communicate with the beings living there. As we grow deeper into the physical world, our memories of the spiritual world are stored further and further away from consciousness under layers of physical memories. The ability to reclaim our understanding of the spiritual part of us is an important skill to learn. How we do this depends on our present spiritual belief system and the path we have chosen to follow. Learning this skill is practicing the tenants of our chosen path. All paths lead to the same place – God. If you have not been following a particular spiritual path, you can practice the *Huna* Way of "no hurt," "service," and "love." These three concepts are the foundations of all other spiritual practices. It is okay to change paths at any time, but remember to stay tolerant of the beliefs and understandings of other individuals. The ability to stay connected to your Higher Self on a daily basis is the key to this skill and practicing higher thoughts, actions and deeds is the measure of mastery.

# THE INNER SELVES AT FIVE YEARS

Five years marks the end of the phase of development known as toddlerhood. The increased maturity of the two minds from age three to five is remarkable. The five year old Selves are more independent and able to make more choices about their life. They are able to play with other children in appropriate ways. They are helpful and usually generous. Their moods are generally happy ones because they have learned how to handle frustrations better. The Selves of this age have discovered they can tolerate stress, express or withhold feelings, approach difficult tasks and succeed, know their own likes and dislikes, and have become more self-aware.

They can also evaluate the requirements of a task and judge whether or not they can accomplish it or need assistance. They are beginning to know their limitations and can use this as motivation for learning new skills. They are more able to think before they act. This skill indicates a further capacity of the *'Uhane* to control the actions of the *'Unihipili*.

---

### Developmental Skills at Five Years

1. The ability to think before acting. ( *'Uhane* skill )

2. The ability to know current limitations, ask for assistance, and know where to go to find other resources. ( *'Uhane* and *'Unihipili* skills )

3. The ability to read in order to learn. ( *'Uhane* and *'Unihipili* skills )

---

120

At five the Selves know that the alphabet is about words. They may even be reading a little. It is an exciting moment when the Selves put together the letters to form the words and understand the concept. Reading opens up a whole new world of learning opportunities for them. Reading is an essential element in higher education.

Some five year old Selves are ready to go to school, and some are not quite ready. Intellectually the *'Uhane* is ready for longer periods of challenge, but physically and emotionally the *'Unihipili* is not ready. The intellectual attention span of the five year old *'Uhane* is about 5 minutes. The physical attention span of the *'Unihipili* may be shorter. The emotional attention span will always be short. Kindergarten is a time to explore these longer periods of concentration and to learn classroom behavior. Half a day spent in Kindergarten is an appropriate length of time for the five year old Selves. The Selves still need to be in the family environment to continue learning.

Toddlerhood comes to an end at age five. The Selves have mastered motor skills; emotional and mental stability; the rudiments of self-discipline; and, are beginning to think before acting. Thy are ready to continue learning in a different setting. Formal education can be either public or private schooling, home schooling, or unschooling. There are advantages and disadvantages to each type. Parents must decide what is appropriate for their child based on their lifestyle, their beliefs, and their financial situation. Whatever educational method is selected, the young Selves are now ready to learn more about the world.

Dorothy Werner, media liaison for the National Homeschool Association, recently commented, "I believe that human beings arrive on this Earth wanting to know absolutely everything, and the best thing we can do as parents is to just get out of the way—just be there to let them know what opportunities are there." Children will learn what they need to know when they are ready. The five year Selves are ready to learn many new things.

# *HUNA* TECHNIQUES FOR MASTERING FIVE YEAR OLD SKILLS

 **The ability to think before acting.**

This ability is an extension of the previous abilities of being able to identify feelings of the Self and others and to differentiate between feelings and actions. It is also an extension of the skill to rein in feelings and control impulses. As the *'Uhane* grows in strength and learns the skill to make decisions and the *'Unihipili* learns to follow the Basic Commands, the Selves will learn to stop and think before acting. This skill extends the laws of cause and effect into the social world. We learn this skill through observation, experimentation and practice. Before making any decision, the *'Uhane* stops the *'Unihipili* and they have a discussion on the ramifications of possible actions. Then the *'Uhane* makes the decision taking into consideration the feelings of the *'Unihipili*. Begin by asking your *'Unihipili* to cooperate and help you remember to stop and discuss any situation before acting. This skill is learned through practice.

 **The ability to know current limitations, ask for assistance, and where to go to find other resources.**

Much of what the Selves will learn in school helps them master this skill. The Selves at five are aware of some of their limitations. They will spend fantasy time portraying great and noble deeds and aspirations. This prepares them for learning their limitations and motivates the Selves to expand the possibilities of doing whatever they desire. Learning to ask for assistance is learning trust, trust of others. Learning where to go to find other resources is an invaluable aid in expanding knowledge. Again we master this skill by practice. Consult with your *'Unihipili* and *'Uhane* and make a list of your current limitations. Make another list of your aspirations and goals. Compare the two lists and note the areas that need assistance. Note the areas that require other resources. Select one aspiration and write down the steps to get there, including how to expand your current limitations and where to go to find other resources to help you. Take action one step at a time and celebrate your success when you reach your goal. Select the next aspiration and follow the same steps to success.

## The ability to read in order to learn.

In our Information Age the ability to read is critical. If you have emotions or thoughts about your ability to read, you may need to master this skill. Slow readers are not stupid, they are more than likely auditory or tactile learners. They may also have dyslexia problems or other associative difficulties. There are many ways to overcome these difficulties. The skill here is to take action as nurturing parents of our Selves and assist them. Go back to the basics. There are several good phonics programs available to purchase and learn in the privacy of your own home. Adult literacy programs are available in most communities. Audio books are good resource, especially if they are played while the Selves look at the written words and follow along. Consult a professional and have a professional evaluation of your reading challenge and follow the recommended therapies. To know your reading ability and take steps to improve it is to master this skill.

# THE DEVELOPMENTAL PHASE OF PRIMARY SCHOOL AGE

## THE INNER SELVES FROM SIX TO EIGHT YEARS

At six years the *'Unihipili* reaches the limit of its emotional age. It will always be the Inner Child, whose emotions remain childlike. The *'Unihipili* must learn to control and raise the emotions to their highest level before it can graduate to become a *'Uhane*. The *'Unihipili* learns how to control the emotions by the interaction with other Selves in the school environment. The beginning of formal schooling has a strong symbolic meaning. School symbolizes the moving from the environment of home and family to the environment of community for the child. To the parents it symbolizes a move toward independence. School becomes a new source of influence as the Selves become less dependent on the parents. This next phase of development is Primary School Age. The world of school provides new opportunities for success and failure, outside evaluation, peer group formations and social opportunities. It provides a broader source of information and experiences. The Selves learn that there are other ways of doing things beside the family way.

The six to eight year old Selves gain the ability to perform logical operations, use and generate categories, manipulate more than one dimension at a time, reward themselves for good behavior, and learn that other Selves do not perceive the world as they do. They gain an understanding of the Ideal Selves, which is a complex view of the future Selves. They will also explore how skills, professions, values, and personal relationships shape the Selves.

One of the major areas of growth of the primary school age Selves is in gender role identification. The Selves acquire more knowledge about gender behavior and expectations. Male and female preferences will develop and the Selves will identify more closely with the parent of the same gender. Parents are role models for girls and boys that provide support for self-esteem and for personal and professional success. The Primary School Age Selves need the right kind of role models to help prepare them for the future.

During this phase of development, the standards and limits of behavior become a part of self-esteem. The specific values of parents will be integrated into moral development. This is the time of parental influence on moral behavior. The *'Uhane* learns moral lessons from his parents. The parents represent the *'Aumakua* to the Selves and it is in this role that they impart wisdom and knowledge about the proper way to live. To *Huna* parents, who have already begun to teach the young Selves the "no hurt" way, it is easy to move this moral model into the new world of school and peers. The moral behavior of children is a reflection of parental

> **Our moral behavior is a reflection of our parents' behavior rather than their words.**

behavior rather than their words. The Selves learn by observing the behavior of their adult models. The strong affectionate bond between parents and the Selves is the most effective force in promoting positive moral behavior.

Self-esteem grows stronger in this phase of development. It is a result of self-evaluation in competence and social acceptance and becomes more discerning as the Selves grow. In the Primary School Age phase, self-esteem is based on how well a *'Unihipili* can perform motor skills appropriate to his age; how well the *'Uhane* applies the thinking process to new academic subjects; and, how well they both use their social skills to be accepted by their peers. The Selves now come under outside evaluation by both peers and teachers.

The Primary School Selves are expected to evaluate a situation and anticipate the consequences of their behavior before they act. Without the proper training to be able to do this in the Toddlerhood phase of development, this is a difficult task to master in this phase. The Selves are also expected to show initiative. "Initiative" is described by Erik Erikson as "active inquiry and investigation." Active inquiry is an element of Will power. The *'Uhane* continues to strengthen its Will over the next five years until it can engage its intention with ease. Young Selves who were allowed to explore

> **Initiative is active inquiry and investigation.**

their world without outside interference develop this initiative naturally

Piaget called the Primary School Age the age of "concrete operational thought." This type of thought includes learning the physical laws of the world. It also includes more concrete views of abstract questions, such as what is good and evil, truth and fiction. Piaget described this kind of thought in terms of developmental skills of conservation, classification, combination, and group play.

---

### Developmental Skills for Primary School Age

1.  **Conservation:** the knowledge that physical matter does not magically appear or disappear.  ( *'Uhane* skill )

2.  **Classification:** the ability to group things according to some dimension they all have in common.  ( *'Uhane* skill )

3.  **Combination:** the ability to manipulate numbers.  ( *'Uhane* and *'Unihipili* skills)

4.  **Group play:** the ability to participate in peer cooperation (games). (*'Unihipili* skill )

---

Primary or elementary schools assist the Selves to further develop tools for learning. They are exposed to a wide range of knowledge, learn new problem solving methods, and are given many opportunities to practice these new skills.  School also offers continuos feedback and provides other adult role models.  The Selves can set personal goals and standards and learn that practice and diligent efforts pay off.

The impact of television and the movies on primary school age Selves is tremendous. The Selves are beginning to differentiate between fantasy and reality, but have not achieved mature discernment.  The violence depicted on television resides in the fantasy world, but becomes very real to the young Selves.  When they see an actor die violently in one program and then see him alive and healthy in the next, there is no understanding about physical death. His *'Unihipili* will only anticipate a thrilling and exciting lifestyle in which he will still be alive no matter what he does.  When violence is all around him, the *'Uhane* does not understand that violence is not okay.  The media message is that violence and killing are perfectly normal behaviors.   These messages add aggressive strategies to a *'Unihipili's* responses.   They narrow the options for the Selves and give them unrealistic

solutions for handling unpleasant situations.   This undermines any kind of training in moral and ethical behavior.

**If the Selves rely on the world of television as their fantasy world, the behavior of the role models they observe is the behavior they will follow.**

> **Fantasy and reality are the same to the Inner Child.**

As a learning tool, television is excellent for providing an incredible range of informational, historical and scientific programs. Some of these programs are appropriate for young Selves, but many of them are only appropriate for adult Selves. Research has proven that adult content programs create anxiety in children. **Remember the *'Unihipili* never gets any older than six years.** There are many types of programs your *'Unihipili* should not be watching, especially violence and horror programs. In fact, *'Unihipili* in this phase of development should be actively participating in life, not learning how to be passive observers. Television viewing is a solitary and passive activity.

The same caution is advised for video and computer games. Unrealistic shooting and killing games provide the same kind of aggressive input into the Selves. To the *'Unihipili* the symbolic figure that gets vaporized in a game doesn't really expire, it just comes back to life again when you start the game over. Fantasy and reality are one and the same to this age. Again these games are solitary activities.

When the *'Uhane* learns to read, independent inquiry begins. A whole new world of imagination, information and possibilities opens up. Parents model good reading habits by reading themselves. Children enjoy reading with their parents. Every *'Uhane* can learn the basics of reading. However, we are not just visual learners, but auditory and tactile learners as well. Some *'Uhane* are more focused

> **We have different modes of learning.**

on the auditory, while others are focused on the tactile. We are all combinations of these three forms of input. These modes of learning and expressing thoughts develop at an earlier age. We can move out of one mode into another, but it takes a conscious awareness. *'Uhane* who are having difficulty in learning how to read are more likely to prefer auditory or tactile modes of learning. These *'Uhane* are not stupid and should never be yelled at or shamed. They need help in shifting to the visual mode **before** reading. They need help in learning the rules of reading, such as looking at the word and sounding out the letters, while staying in the visual mode. We need to be aware that our *'Uhane* learn in different modes and help them learn how to shift these modes as needed.

It is not too early to begin talking to the Selves about the dangers of drugs, alcohol and smoking. Remember the Selves learn by observing and imitating their parents. If you drink, take drugs or smoke, you are teaching the young Selves to do the same. It is not okay to hurt yourself.

The Primary School Age is a time for peer interaction. As much emotional learning occurs on the playground as intellectual learning occurs in the classroom. The interactions and lessons experienced by the Selves in the toddlerhood world of fantasy are now acted out in the world of school. Social learning is a major focus of this phase of development. New rules for behavior at school and in social situations are learned and integrated into the Selves.

# *HUNA* TECHNIQUES FOR MASTERING PRIMARY SCHOOL AGE SKILLS

 **Conservation: the knowledge that physical matter does not magically appear and disappear.**

This skill is the beginning of the mastery of the formal physical laws of matter. This skill is the ability of the Selves to distinguish the world of matter from the other worlds. Being able to use the laws of any particular world is a necessary skill to be able to exist in that world. We begin here in the physical world by learning science. Most of us have learned the laws of the physical world, but if we haven't mastered the fundamental laws of physics it is our responsibility to learn those laws. We do this through the study of basic science. Take classes, do internet studies or read elementary science books. Since we live in the physical world during our time on earth it is important to understand how it works. From basic science move into the fascinating subject of quantum physics. There are many excellent books available about the latest discoveries in quantum physics written for the non-scientist. Quantum physics bridges the physical and spiritual worlds.

 **Classification: the ability to group things according to some dimension they all have in common.**

This skill is the ability of the *'Unihipili* to see patterns and associations. It begins early in Toddlerhood and is refined during the Primary School Age. The *'Uhane* participates in this skill by categorizing the patterns. As the two work together, they expand their ability to classify. If you have difficulty is classifying, you can learn this skill by practicing. There are many games and books available to teach you how to classify. Play games with your *'Unihipili* to identify patterns and classify all kinds of objects.

 **Combination: the ability to manipulate numbers.**

The ability to manipulate numbers is secondary to the ability to read. Even though we have calculators and computers to manipulate numbers faster and more correctly, the Selves still need to understand the basics of mathematics. Mathematics is a language of the physical world and expands the physical comprehension level of the Selves. If you have difficulty with numbers, then you may need to master this skill. Bypass the handy calculator and regularly practice the basic skills of addition, subtraction, multiplication, and division.

> **Group play:  the ability to participate in peer cooperation.**

This skill involves more than just playing games.  It involves the ability of the *'Unihipili* to interact with other Selves and the ability of the *'Uhane* to guide appropriate social behavior.  If you have emotions or thoughts centered around participating in peer activities or groups, you may need to master this skill.  It requires the cooperation of both Selves.  Elementary lessons of social interaction are easy, but they take action.  Here are the basic steps for interacting with others:

1. **Speak directly to others when spoken to.**
2. **Initiate social contact, don't always wait for others.**
3. **Carry on conversations beyond "yes" and "no."**
4. **Express gratitude toward others.**
5. **Let someone else go first.**
6. **Wait until you are served.**
7. **Use "thank you" and "please" and other good manners.**

If your *'Unihipili* is shy, you may need to master this skill. Start practicing one step at a time, until that behavior feels comfortable, then go on to the next step.  It won't be long before you can participate fully in any group.

# THE DEVELOPMENTAL PHASE OF MIDDLE SCHOOL AGE

## THE INNER SELVES FROM NINE TO TWELVE YEARS

The Middle School Age phase of development covers nine to twelve years. This phase focuses on intellectual growth, competence, and a growing investment in work. The Selves learn the fundamental skills of culture that are valued by their society. As the Selves gain confidence in these skills, they begin to have a more realistic image of their own potential contribution to the larger community. They begin to identify their Purpose. In our society, "school" is the means by which we pass on the wisdom and skills of past generations. The Selves learn much from the formal school experience.

The Selves also need opportunity to be with the Elders of their family to learn from their wisdom and experience. The Selves learn more than just information from the Elders, they also learn respect, honor, and love. Grandparents and members of the older generation are valuable resources. The Elders become the wiser and nonjudgmental representatives of the 'Aumakua in the lives of younger family members.

During this time the Selves will make their first personal commitment to a social group outside the family, such as a youth group. Groups such as the Girl and Boy Scouts, YMCA, Boys and Girls Clubs, or church youth groups, all offer the Selves of this phase a broader range of social experiences through the interaction with their peers and other adult role models.

The daily interaction of the Selves in school with their peers brings a greater appreciation of many different points of view. Peer groups consist of children of the same gender. They explore together what it means to be female or male. The Selves at this phase become more sensitive to peer pressure. In fact, the need for peer approval becomes a very powerful force in their lives. They also experience a special kind of intimacy with their same-gender friends. This is the time of "best friends," some of which they will keep for the rest of their lives. All of these experiences move the Selves through the developmental skills for this phase.

---

### Developmental Skills for Middle School Age

1. **Social cooperation: the ability to relate in appropriate ways in a group. (*'Unihipili* skill)**

2. **Self-evaluation: the ability to set realistic goals and assess own progress. ( *'Uhane* skill )**

3. **Skill learning: the improvement of physical, artistic, and intellectual skills. ( *'Uhane* and *'Unihipili* skills)**

4. **Team playing: the ability to be responsible for specific actions within a group setting. ( *'Uhane* and *'Unihipili* skills)**

---

Through the group experience the Selves shift their focus from self-centered to other-centered. Social cooperation teaches the *'Uhane* about acceptable group behavior and expression. It teaches the *'Unihipili* about sharing feelings and experiences with others. It is important for the Selves to experience the peer group. The members are usually on the same level. It gives the Selves power, status, and access to more resources. The Selves form a close bond with the other members of the peer group and they want to spend more time away from home with these new friends.

**We make self-evaluations based on skills and responsibilities.**

The Selves are now able to make self-evaluations based on their new skills and responsibilities. They also make these evaluations based on how their teachers see them, how the parents see them, and how the peer group sees them. With self-evaluation comes the ability of the *'Uhane* to set realistic goals and assess its own progress towards those goals without outside assistance. An example of this is completing homework assignments without being told.

The most impressive skills in this phase are in the artistic, athletic and intellectual areas. The artistic skills blossom during this time, especially those in music. Many children begin instrumental music lessons in this phase. Music is a different language to be learned and both the *'Uhane* and *'Unihipili* must work together to master it. The *'Uhane* has to conceptualize the placement of the fingers and correct method to play the instrument before the *'Unihipili* can control the physical aspects of the body to achieve the correct sounds. This musical ability helps the Selves sing in harmony, write original music, play in orchestras, and sing in choirs. Music is a form of expression for the *'Unihipili* and will continue to be used as such throughout the life of the human. Exposure to all kinds of musical expression is critical to musical skill. By mastering other languages and their cultural concepts the *'Uhane* learns to think in different ways. Music is as much a language as is mathematics.

> **Music is another language to be learned and shared.**

Intellectual skills continue to improve in this phase. The Selves can grasp fundamental principles of problems and solve them. Individual differences in children of this age become more apparent. Parents should celebrate such diversity and allow each pair of Selves to develop its own styles, talents and abilities.

Fundamental attitudes about work are established at this time. If the Selves are yelled at to complete their work, their attitude will not be positive. As the Selves develop these new skills and personal standards, they evolve an initial assessment of their possible contributions to society. They begin to get a sense of what their Purpose is all about and how they can use their Purpose for a fulfilling life.

Research has proven that the expectations of teachers, coaches, youth group leaders and parents effect a child's learning abilities. The *'Unihipili* is especially sensitive to the psychic communication of thoughts and images from these powerful figures. The *'Unihipili* will share this information with the *'Uhane,* who will then base its expectations and abilities on this nonverbal evaluation. Adults should guard against sending these negative thoughts as they influence their own behavior toward the Selves. Each Self is fully capable and intelligent and should be treated as such.

Team playing teaches the Selves early lessons on social interdependence, how to rely on other Selves, and the value of dividing tasks within the group. Team sports teach the value and nature of competition, both the negative and positive sides. The Selves learn that it is in the best interest of the team as a whole if each member is strong and improves that strength. They learn that each position has a unique function and the team's best chance of winning depends on each person performing his or her own function. The Selves also learn the value and consequences of their actions for the whole group.

> **Each position on a team has its unique function.**

The *'Uhane* learns to conceptualize the athletic movements of the game, the strategies, and its unique function within the team. The *'Unihipili* learns to refine the physical movements of the body and add positive emotion for better performance. The *'Unihipili* also learns loyalty to a cause, coordination, timing, concentration, and cooperation. The Selves learn the value of caring for the physical body, building good physical health, and the importance of stamina. Good sports experiences are beneficial for the Selves in this phase. However, there are negative aspects to athletics in the form of ignorant coaches who yell and batter the self-esteem of the young Selves. Many Selves avoid the learning experiences of sports because of the negative aspects.

It is quite appropriate to teach sex education to Middle School Age children. Some girls have already started their periods by age 11. It is important to learn about sex before the onset of puberty. Children need to have both school and parental education about sex. The *'Unihipili* needs the information **before** the increased hormonal activity distorts the emotions. The *'Uhane* needs the information in order to recognize the source of such emotional upheaval in order to help the *'Unihipili* handle the changes. Sex education should include information on the biological functions of all life forms. It should also include the larger picture of human evolution. A discussion of different cultural celebrations of maturity and the importance of these rituals and ceremonies should be part of this education. The significance of moving from childhood to adulthood in terms of physical, emotional, mental, and spiritual changes should be discussed.

The emotional implications of sex are important for a child to know. The *'Unihipili* needs to know about the psychological and healing dimensions of love. This knowledge, for example, prepares a young person to make more appropriate choices at the proper times. The

'*Uhane* learns that sexual closeness is a way of communicating love, as well as a way to produce children. The Selves need to understand that sexual closeness is a way of creating energy, an energy that is shared best between committed partners.

> **Sex education should include information on the biological functions of all life forms.**

Both Selves need to know about the epidemics of sexually transmitted diseases and how crucial it is to personal health to avoid dangerous situations. The facts of modern living include the real possibility of contracting the AIDS virus. It will be years before medical science finds a cure and preventative vaccine for AIDS. Until then, the Selves must have the information they need to protect them. Information alone cannot protect the young Selves. They must be taught strategies to cope with the overwhelming feelings of puberty. Giving the Selves practice in making positive choices early in life helps prepare them to make more important choices in adolescence. Parents must also teach strategies which the Selves can use to avoid potentially dangerous situations.

Middle School Age is a time of preparation to handle the adult changes that will soon be evident. It is a time for exploring the artistic dimensions of life. It is a time to learn musical expression. It is also a time to be involved in social groups and team sports and experience new ways of thinking and acting. As the Selves become more aware of their natural abilities and talents, their Purpose begins to unfold.

# *HUNA* TECHNIQUES FOR MASTERING MIDDLE SCHOOL AGE SKILLS

> **Social cooperation: the ability to relate in appropriate ways in a group.**

This skill is one the Selves will use to interact with all kinds of social groups throughout the rest of their lives. It helps the Selves shift from ego-centric to other-centered. It is the ability to care for and help other people. We need the ability to express ourselves in group situations in order to share our knowledge and wisdom with other Selves. And we need to learn knowledge and wisdom from them. We are here to learn and work together towards a better world. If you have emotions or thoughts centered around relating to groups, you may need to master this skill. You master this skill by observation, experimentation and repetition, as well as imitation. You can only do this by being in a group. Choose one group to join and observe the other members, their behavior, and how they participate. Imitate their behavior and experiment by participating in an activity. As the *'Unihipili* gains self-esteem and experience in a group setting and the *'Uhane* learns proper group behavior, the skill will be mastered. This skill is vital to finding your Purpose in life. Purpose usually involves service to others.

> **Self-evaluation: the ability to set realistic goals and assess own progress.**

The *'Uhane* sees the bigger picture for the Selves. From its perspective of logic and the ability to see future consequences, it can set realistic goals. Evaluation is learned from observing the evaluation strategies of others. Self-evaluation is to be done without judgments or criticism. It is to be done with the view of studying certain actions or inactions. If you are not able to set realistic goals and assess your own progress, you may need to master this skill. You begin by setting a goal, working toward it, and assessing your progress without criticizing either Self. Many of us don't practice setting goals and just live on a day to day basis. Goal setting is an important part of the prayer process, for without the ability to set a goal we cannot form a correct picture for the prayer pattern. Setting and achieving goals is our way of measuring success in the physical world.

> **Skill learning: the improvement of physical, artistic, and intellectual skills.**

The ability of the Selves to improve skills is an important ability. Often we stop at a particular plateau or don't attempt something because someone told us we couldn't. Moving beyond those impediments is the mastery of this skill. If you are stuck at some level on any physical, artistic, or intellectual skill, you may need to master self-improvement. To improve, you must move forward. If you do not play an instrument, take lessons and master the basics. If you do not paint, draw, or create artistically, take lessons or teach yourself. If you have not attempted any intellectual improvements, choose an area and begin. The skill is to master learning and the only way to achieve it is to take action.

> **Team playing: the ability to be responsible for specific actions within a group setting.**

This skill is closely connected to the first developmental skill of Middle School Age of social cooperation. This skill moves beyond social interaction to participating in a meaningful way in the group. It involves being responsible for certain actions. In sports groups this means the *'Unihipili* and *'Uhane* work together to play their position and not interfere with any other position. It means they refine and improve their physical skills to become the best player in that position. In other groups it means volunteering for a job and doing the best you can to fulfill the responsibilities of that job. It means doing new jobs and learning new skills. Team playing aids the Selves in building trust, responsibility, and reliability with other Selves. It also helps the Selves recognize possible aspects of their Purpose. To master this skill you must join a sports or other kind of group and actively participate. It is through action that we learn.

# THE DEVELOPMENTAL PHASE OF TEEN AGE ADOLESCENCE

## THE INNER SELVES FROM TWELVE TO SEVENTEEN YEARS

"Adolescence is a time of gradual evolution of a self-concept that is in harmony with the family and the culture," state Barbara and Philip Newman. This phase of development spans the onset of puberty to graduation from high school. Teenage Adolescents need their parents as much as Toddlers, especially the parent of the same gender. This phase is characterized by rapid physical changes, significant conceptual maturation, and a heightened sensitivity to peer pressures. These changes bring adolescents closer to a clearer image of themselves as adults. The changes to the *'Uhane* have been remarkable. It has now reached its full strength and should be able to control the actions of the *'Unihipili*. The *'Unihipili* has learned cooperation and is struggling to stabilize the hormones and the accompanying mood shifts of puberty. During this phase of development the *'Uhane* learns how to be a proper guide and teacher to the *'Unihipili* through associating with the parent of the same gender. The *'Uhane* has reached what Plato called the Age of Reason.

As soon as the Selves learn to drive, parents have fewer opportunities to guide or influence them. The Selves become totally mobile and can go anywhere they choose. They spend even more time away from home with friends, in a part-time job, or at sports or school events. Conflicts over choices made by the Selves often create tension between the child and the parents. If parents have been using love and logic discipline and have given the child's *'Uhane* practice in making good choices, there is less conflict. The parents will already trust the Selves to make good choices. The *'Unihipili* does not want conflict and always wants to move toward resolution. Both Selves have a great desire for peace.

The greatest motivation in this phase is the quest for answers to the big questions of "who am I?" "what am I supposed to be doing?" and "with whom do I belong?" The *'Uhane* realizes it must establish its own values for the best and highest good of both Selves. As the Selves reach for more independence and autonomy, they must have personal values to be able to branch out on their own. Rebellion is a symptom of this process of establishing adult values and using them in personal choices. The *'Uhane* of both parents must be able to step aside now and give full control to the child's *'Uhane*. The child's *'Uhane* must be able to make her own decisions. The degree in which the parents allow the Selves to assume adult-like roles in the family and make more adult choices influences their successful transition into adulthood.

---

## Developmental Skills of Teen Age Adolescence

1. **Formal operational thought: the ability to conceptualize about variables. (** *'Uhane* **skill )**

2. **Physical maturation: the ability to handle adult changes to the body. (** *'Unihipili* **skill )**

3. **Membership in a peer group: the ability to be accepted while holding onto personal values. (** *'Uhane* **and** *'Unihipili* **skills )**

4. **Partnering relationships: the ability to relate to the Selves of another. (** *'Uhane* **and** *'Unihipili* **skills )**

---

The developmental skills associated with this age are more complex and difficult. The Selves in this phase are more flexible, more critical, and have a more abstract view of the world. The *'Uhane* can manipulate more than two categories of variables at one time, i.e., speed, distance and time. They can conceptualize changes in the future. They can hypothesize about logical sequences of events that might happen. And most importantly, the *'Uhane* can conceptualize the consequences of actions. Deductive thought has matured.

Piaget describes this new ability as "formal operational thought." It is the ability to conceptualize about variables, which interact simultaneously. It is the next step in higher intellectual ability. Understanding advanced science and philosophy are good examples of this increased intellectual ability. The *'Uhane* can now generate a hypothesis about events which the *'Unihipili* has never perceived through its senses.

This is the time when the future becomes a real part of the life of the Selves. This is an important step for *Huna* students, for it is this ability to conceptualize the future and the consequences of future actions that is necessary for the prayer process and for living the "no hurt" life. The *'Uhane* must be able to evaluate future consequences in terms of potential hurts in order to prepare a proper prayer. The *'Uhane* must also be able to refrain from selecting a future that might hurt the Selves or the Selves of others.

The *'Uhane* has learned to appreciate the world and accepted the diversity of its cultures. This is important for as the adolescent reaches adulthood, the Selves must be able to be <u>inclusive</u> instead of <u>exclusive</u>. The adolescent has also learned how to function in different roles. This ability started at age three with the beginning of fantasy play. This fantasy play prepared the Selves to play certain roles in the adult world. Each role exerts a specific demand on a person as he fulfills the different roles of child, student, worker, teammate and friend. As the Selves become more selective of the roles they play, they are better able to maintain balance.

**Patience is a necessary strategy for controlling hormonal changes.**

Physical and emotional maturation is the hallmark of this phase. The expansion and exchange of information in our technological age has greatly intensified the experiences of this phase of development, especially in terms of sexual experimentation. Very few young people over the age of 19 have abstained from sexual intercourse. This phase of development is a critical time for both boys and girls. The physical development leads to a heightened awareness of body sensations. The Adolescent Selves naturally experiment with physical and emotional arousal. They are discovering a new kind of raw energy – sexual energy and the *'Unihipili* wants to play. Some Adolescents use this new energy experience to escape or avoid reality. Some adults continue to use this sexual energy as an escape. As with all other aspects of learning, repetition and experimentation teach the Selves about sex. Unfortunately, there are some aspects of sexual learning that are dangerous and not available to the Selves at this age. The most important strategy the *'Uhane* can use at this point is to teach the *'Unihipili* patience. Patience to wait until the hormones stabilize. Patience to wait until the sexual emotions balance. Patience to wait until one finds the right partner with which to experience a mature and fulfilling sexual intimacy.

Teen Age Adolescence is the time when the Selves need the guidance and support of the same gender parent. They need adequate and accurate information about the physical, emotional, mental and spiritual development of adults. They need to be able to experience and accept these changes in an atmosphere of family and peer support. Often information they receive from their peers or other adults is inadequate or incomplete or does not answer their specific questions. It is through the association with the same gender parent that they gain needed information about manhood and womanhood. Girls need their mothers to become women. Boys need their fathers to become men.

Unfortunately, many fathers are not available to their sons. In most single-family homes the father is the missing parent. And worse, our society has abandoned single mothers to raise their sons alone. In other cultures boys without fathers have older brothers, uncles, cousins, and grandfathers to help them through this important phase of development. In America, boys have other boys. Without the resource of their fathers, young adolescent boys are "morally neglected" and left to find their way alone. They are bombarded with violence, overtly sexual messages, and aggression on TV, in the streets, and through their music.

It is a great sadness that boys have to grow up without their fathers.

It is a great sadness in our society that "the vast majority of children who commit crimes, are murdered, wind up in prison, suffer physical abuse, commit suicide, go homeless, need foster care, or are drug or alcohol addicts, are boys." These comments are quoted from Michael Gurian, family therapist and author, in his most recent book, *The Good Son: Shaping the Moral Development of Our Boys and Young Men.* Gurian agrees with Tine Thevenin that boys are indeed inherently different from girls biologically, emotionally and mentally. He has studied cultures all over the world and concluded "cultures have always known that elders are the ones to train the young males in how to live their lives." He believes that the lack of fathers and other older males in the lives of boys is one of the top three problems in our culture. Our culture does not have a formal rite that marks a clear distinction between boyhood and manhood. Some young masculine Selves don't make the transition to manhood until they are over thirty.

Physical maturation for girls occurs two years earlier than for boys. Girls in today's society are concerned, and often obsessed, about "getting fat" as their bodies redistribute weight in more womanly proportions. Our culture correlates thinness with beauty. The media has set the standard for female beauty for any age as blonde hair, long legs, large bust, and a tall and extremely skinny body. Girls need to maintain a well-balanced diet, regular exercise and drink plenty of fresh water in order for their *'Unihipili* to be able to cope with the physical changes.

Girls need early discussions and guidance on the dangers of repressing the natural growth of their bodies during adolescence.

Girls need the guidance of their mothers during this phase. Most mothers work outside the home and have little time to share with their daughters. Girls need acceptance and support as they move from girlhood to womanhood. Girls, who have little opportunity for positive identification with their mothers, will not acquire the skills they need to become a responsible and fulfilled woman. Girls in other cultures become women with the onset of menses. These girls have already received all the training they need to take their places in society. In some cultures girls of this age are ready to marry and bear children. In the Western world, girls have no rites of passage and have not been given the proper training and information they need to make responsible choices. Some girls get pregnant at an early age and are forced into the role of mother before they are ready.

> **Girls need their mothers to help them become women.**

The last developmental skill for this phase is membership in a peer group. This is the age of the Mall Experience and experimentation with image. The Selves of this age want to be different, and they are all different -- together. Peer pressure becomes stronger at this age. In fact, the peer group often has more influence over the Selves than the parents do. Peer groups offer support, comfort and security for the Selves, especially when there are conflicts in the home. They offer status, friendship and intimacy. The intimacy experienced in a peer group prepares the Selves for intimacy in other relationships. Conflicts between the values of the family and the values of the peer group prepare the Selves to establish their own values. Parents should remember that peer groups are a necessary learning experience during this phase.

> **This is the age of the Mall Experience and image experimentation.**

This is the last opportunity that parents have to teach their children everything they need to know as an adult. The Selves need to know more than what they learn in school. They need to know all the things necessary to live as an adult. They need to know how to take care of their *'Uhane* and *'Unihipili*, how to be good parents, and how to be good nurturers. They need to know about the world of spirit and how to integrate the spiritual into their lives.

# *HUNA* TECHNIQUES FOR MASTERING TEEN AGE ADOLESCENT SKILLS

> **Formal operational thought: the ability to conceptualize about variables.**

This skill is the ability to conceptualize the future. It involves being able to predict consequences of thoughts and actions based on what the *'Uhane* has learned about the laws of the physical world. It takes practice to master this skill. The best way to learn it is to do it. Set a possible goal and then visualize the consequences of the actions necessary to achieve the goal. For example, if you would like a new job, set that as your goal. Ask and answer questions such as "if I had a new job would I live in this same area? What would the hours be and would I be willing to work those hours? Would I need to take classes in order to qualify for this new job?" When you can visualize different consequences, decide which are acceptable, and which you are willing to experience, you have mastered this skill.

> **Physical maturation: the ability to handle adult changes to the body.**

Physical maturation comes before emotional maturation in our society. We are constantly pressured to remain emotionally immature. All around us are messages to indulge in impulsive behavior, to ignore the plight of our fellow humans, and take what we want. Maturity requires our *'Unihipili* to be Emotionally Intelligent and our *'Uhane* to be Intellectually Intelligent with the ability and skill to discern and reject. To master this skill the *'Unihipili* must master the elements of Emotional Intelligence: the ability to control emotional impulses; the ability to read another's innermost feelings; and, the ability to handle relationships smoothly. The *'Uhane* must be able to be a good guide and teacher to the *'Unihipili*. This means the two Selves work together to learn patience and concentrate on knowing what the other person is feeling. These strategies are the basis of all adult intimate relationships. You learn this skill by practicing patience in some situations and practicing emotional skills in all situations.

**Membership in a peer group: the ability to be accepted while holding onto personal values.**

Membership in a group does not necessarily mean you have to accept all the values of the governing board members. Personal values and integrity are the skills to master here. Peer groups give us the opportunity to construct and test our personal values. In order to master these skills, you have to be a member of a peer group. Some Selves prefer to be members of groups where the ages are either older or younger. They are avoiding the opportunities to master this peer group skill. Join a group of people of your same age. Be an active member and openly express your personal values in appropriate ways at appropriate times. The learning technique is the same, observation, experimentation and repetition. Mastery requires you to take action, not remain a passive observer.

**Partnering relationships: the ability to relate to the Selves of another.**

This skill begins with family members and moves on to persons of the same gender and finally to persons of the opposite gender. The skill to be a good partner begins at this phase with best friends. To be a good friend means to be accepting, nonjudgmental, tolerant, loving, kind, courteous, and interested. To master this skill, you have to practice it. Many *'Unihipili* are afraid to reach out to others in a more intimate way. These *'Unihipili* need to be encouraged, supported and loved. They need help from the *'Uhane* to make a new friend and begin to practice the elements of this skill. Friendships are cultivated and take time and energy. Make a new friend today. "To have a friend, you must be a friend."

# THE DEVELOPMENTAL PHASE OF MATURE ADOLESCENCE

## THE INNER SELVES FROM SEVENTEEN TO TWENTY-TWO YEARS

This phase of development is considered the final phase of childhood in Western society. In the Mature Adolescence phase, the Selves will be compelled to make relatively permanent choices about their own life including occupation or career, a personal code, a partner or spouse, political ideology, and the spiritual path. In many other world cultures these decisions have already been made, sometimes by the child's parents and sometimes by the child. In our society the Selves make these personal decisions.

The developmental skills for the Mature Adolescent Selves include a continuation of higher education or certification in a trade. Without this important training the Selves cannot bring financial success into their life, nor will they be able to move away from survival mode to fulfillment of Purpose.

From this point onward, the Selves work together to accomplish developmental skills. Integration has taken place with the *'Uhane* in control, making decisions based on logic and emotional input from the *'Unihipili*. The *'Uhane* has reached its intellectual maturity at age 20. The spiritual aspects of the personality are firmly established. For *Huna* students, this integration also includes the presence of the *'Aumakua* in the life of the person.

144

---

**Development Skills for Mature Adolescents**

1. **Autonomy from parents: the ability to embrace independence.**
   ( *'Uhane* and *'Unihipili* skills )

2. **Gender role identity: the choice of lifestyle.** ( *'Uhane* and *'Unihipili* skills )

3. **Internalized morality: the ability to follow a spiritual path.**
   ( *'Uhane* and *'Unihipili* skills)

4. **Formulating Purpose: the ability to know where you are going.**
   ( *'Uhane* and *'Unihipili* skills )

---

Autonomy and independence come at different times for the Mature Adolescent Selves. Independence occurs when they go off to college, get married early, move out of the family home, or take a job in another town. Independence also occurs if they join the military service. With independence and autonomy the parents begin to relate in new ways to their children. Both parent and child must let go of the old ways and establish a new relationship based on a mutual and loving <u>adult</u> foundation. Some parents do not want to let go of the old relationship. Some children want to hang on to childhood and not move forward into the new adult world. It is crucial to the development of the Selves that the relationship changes.

Gender role identities become firmly integrated in this phase. For boys, being a man involves the ability to hold a steady job, provide for his family if he is married, and be competitive in leisure and business. For girls, being a woman involves the ability to hold a steady job, nurture her family if she is married, and be a homemaker. For Selves who have discovered they are gay or lesbian, this phase of development is more difficult. They may have already admitted they have a different sexual orientation and are struggling with self-acceptance. Now they face the difficult task of communicating this fact with their parents, friends, and family. They are fearful about the direction of their lives, how they will fit into society, and how they will find a partner. As parents, we love our children no matter what the circumstances. We represent the *'Aumakua* on the earthly plane and as such we always give our children unconditional love and our full support.

> **We always love and support our Selves and our children.**

The Selves are now governed by their own moral beliefs. This internalized morality becomes a mature and integrated system that guides their behavior, particularly in the face of strong pressures. This mature system aids the *'Uhane* in exercising choices in matters of greater complexity. The world is no longer "black and white" and choices now involve other considerations. If the Selves have been taught the *Huna* way of "no hurt," these choices are easier to make. The *'Uhane* is able to guide the *'Unihipili* toward a more meaningful experience of life.

Career choices represent a direct or indirect expression of the internal value system. Experimentation with different occupations is one way to select a career. The Selves often take jobs that give them experience in many fields, before selecting one that fits their needs and desires. Early jobs in fast food restaurants, gas stations, libraries, mall shops, etc., help establish personal likes and dislikes. Continuing education after high school is important. In the modern world, degrees and technical certification programs are critical to the financial success of a person. The Selves may also explore other career alternatives such as the Peace Corps, exchange programs, or the military. Parents can support the Selves by encouraging experimentation and higher education opportunities.

As the Selves choose a career, they formulate their Purpose. Identifying Purpose and putting it into action is an important skill at this phase of development. For some, Purpose has been clear for a long time. For others, it is more difficult to identify. Parents assist the Selves by modeling their own Purposes. A child's Purpose is the synthesis of the Purposes of the parents. Some parents have not yet acquired the skill of finding their own Purpose. We need Purpose as a guide to living.

> **We need Purpose for fulfillment.**

# *HUNA* TECHNIQUES FOR MASTERING MATURE ADOLESCENT SKILLS

**Autonomy from parents: the ability to embrace independence.**

The skills for the Mature Adolescent phase are combined skills for both the *'Uhane* and the *'Unihipili.* At this age, the Selves have learned how to work together to achieve success. Independent living is the goal. The Three Selves become an Inner Family. Embracing independence does not mean giving up past relationships. It means the Selves now make their own decisions independent from the parents' authority. They still appreciate and seek out advice and consul from parents and other adult mentors, but the decisions and their consequences are made independently by the Selves. This skill is learned first by making the decision to leave home. Then to actively find a place to live and be financially responsible. It means to pack personal belongings and physically move to the new life. Parents help children learn this important skill by supporting their decision for independence and encouraging early decision making. If you have not embraced independence, you can master this skill only by taking action to be responsible for your life.

**Gender role identity: the choice of lifestyle.**

Lifestyles are changing. Humans are exploring new, and perhaps more meaningful, family relationships. The nuclear family is expanding to include intentional families, same gender families, housemates, and unmarried partners. The Selves must choose their lifestyle. The key to this skill is making the choice. Some Selves experiment with different lifestyles before finding the one in which they are the most comfortable. Parents can be encouraging and supportive and accepting. This skill is mastered through careful thought, planning, and action. The *'Uhane* and *'Unihipili* must both agree to and be comfortable with the lifestyle.

**Internalized morality: the ability to follow a spiritual path.**

Some Selves follow a private spiritual path. Others participate in organized religion. Whatever the spiritual path, the ability to follow it is an important skill. Internal morality comes from the influence of the parents, the Spirit that arises from within the *'Unihipili,* and the research and study of the *'Uhane*. Morals and ethics are guidelines for living. The Selves develop personal morality at an earlier age and learn how to put it into practice at this age. Living our beliefs gives us strength, power, and the ability to be tolerant of other beliefs. If you don't have a spiritual path, find one to follow. Read about beliefs and religions. Have discussions with people of different faiths. Select one that speaks to both your Selves and actively participate in personal practices and the faith community.

**Formulating Purpose: the ability to know where you are going.**

Purpose is the framework of living. It is the goal we came to achieve. Each of us has a unique Purpose and important message for the world. In this phase, the Selves formulate their Purpose and begin to fulfill it. How do we find our Purpose? For some Selves, Purpose has been very clear from an early age. For others, it swirls around in the depths of the *'Unihipili* and at the edge of consciousness waiting to be articulated by the *'Uhane*. To discover clues to the nature of our Purpose we look at the Purposes of our individual parents. The first step is to describe in one or two words the Purpose of your mother and the Purpose of your Father. Your Purpose is a synthesis of these two Purposes raised to a higher more spiritual level. Take some time to reflect on the lives of your mother and father. Reflect on your life, your hopes, dreams, desires. State your life's Purpose in a short sentence. It is similar to writing down a mission statement for a business. Purpose guides your life, helps you make decisions, keeps you focused on the important things. Post your Purpose in several prominent places so you can read it and remember it every day. Let your Purpose guide all your decisions.

# THE DEVELOPMENTAL PHASE OF EARLY ADULTHOOD

## THE INNER SELVES FROM TWENTY-TWO TO THIRTY YEARS

This is the time in the life of the Selves in which they claim their rightful place in adult society. They are no longer bound by the rules, values and wishes of their parents, but are able to make choices and suffer the own consequences. In early adulthood young men focus more on occupation and politics. Young women focus on family and religion. Developmental skills are learned by both the *'Unihipili* and *'Uhane*.

Developmental skills for Early Adulthood center around choosing balanced roles. Most adult Selves will marry and begin raising children in this phase. They will commit to a career and a lifestyle that builds self-esteem and social status.

---

### Developmental Skills for Early Adulthood

1. **Work: the ability to choose a fulfilling career.**

2. **Marriage or partnering: the ability to find a suitable person with whom to learn intimacy.**

3. **Child bearing and rearing: the ability to be good nurturers.**

---

Young men and women have now graduated from college or other formal training and begin their careers. For the next several years, the Selves will be competing for advancement opportunities, additional education, and work experience. They may change jobs several times before finding the position that is right for them. Work will become all consuming at this time of life. For some Selves higher education has not been an option and they find themselves in jobs that are low paying or they don't like. Life is more difficult for these Selves. Moving away from work-as-survival to work-as-fulfillment is an important skill to learn. It takes self-knowledge of skills and talents, a plan, persistence, and an understanding of Purpose.

Marriage or partnering usually occurs in this phase in response to biological and social pressures. Marriage or partnering is the school for learning about intimacy between the masculine and feminine Selves. Similarities in personal characteristics, social class, and cultural and religious backgrounds form the basis of most partnerships, despite the common belief that physical attraction is the basis. In early adulthood, the Selves look for intimate relationships, while not fully understanding what intimacy involves. The first years of a marriage or partnership are spent in mutual adaptation. This adaptation includes such things are mutually satisfying sexual relations, sleep patterns, agreement about expenditures and savings, food preferences, and toilet habits.

## Marriage is the school for learning intimacy with two other Selves.

Divorce usually occurs in the first two to four years of marriage because the adaptation is not successful. One or the other of the partners' Selves is not willing to work towards the greater good of the relationship. Research has proven that a psychological commitment must take place before the marriage will be successful. This means that the *'Unihipili* of each partner be committed to the marriage. Most *'Unihipili* don't fully accept their vows until they have tested the relationship. The *'Unihipili* often use impulsive emotional behavior to test the other person's Selves. As each test is passed, the Selves grow closer, trust each other more, and become increasingly sensitive to the feelings and responses of each *'Unihipili*. Without trust, any future growth in the relationship is seriously thwarted.

Intimacy is the result of the interaction between the Selves of each partner. The two *'Uhane* and two *'Unihipili* are exploring the personalities, tastes, and sensitivity of the others. If either of the *'Uhane* is not mature, the marriage will fail. If either of the *'Unihipili* does not know how to trust and love, the marriage will fail. If the partners do not share the same faith or refuse to tolerate spiritual diversity, the marriage will fail. The most successful marriages

150

happen between two fully integrated human beings, who understand the nature of the emotional and intellectual Selves and how to work with them in love.

> ## The most successful marriages are between integrated Selves.

Surprisingly, the success of any marriage depends primarily on the husband's successful emotional maturity and his integration of the Selves. His success includes knowing how to be a responsible male adult. It also includes the stability of his masculine identity; his educational level; his socioeconomic status; and, the happiness of his parents' marriage. It is critical that boys have good adult male role models. Women have to adapt more in a marriage relationship. Fortunately, their gender characteristics allow them to be more adaptable. This does not mean that they should adapt to abusive relationships. Girls need good adult female role models, who are successful.

With marriage and partnering comes the important decision about children. Both partners must agree to have children or not to have children. Some Selves wait for several years after the marriage and just enjoy the intimacy of the relationship before starting a family. Other couples may choose not to have any children. Many younger couples agree to marry because a child has already announced his arrival. These couples may be faced with financial, emotional, mental and social problems before they are ready. The first child brings additional stress to the partners. The decisions necessary for a couple to make together regarding child rearing practices will call on all the skills of the Selves. The decision to marry or partner and to have children are two of the most important decisions the Selves make in their lifetime and should not be entered into lightly or impulsively.

## Two important life decisions: to marry and have children.

151

If the Selves have been nurtured in positive ways by their parents, they will become good nurturers to their children. If they have been abused, they will be abusive to their children. The parenting and nurturing style of a family is passed down to the next generation. However, aware Selves can stop any negative generational practices and replace them with positive, nurturing practices. It is the responsibility of the Selves to provide a good environment and be nurturing parents for their offspring. They become, in turn, representatives of the *'Aumakua* to the young Selves.

Choosing a lifestyle in this phase depends on a number of factors: the preferences of the Selves, the number of people living together, the financial resources of the Selves, the goals for the future, and the development of the skills necessary to succeed. Lifestyles change as the Selves move from one phase to the next. Material possessions become more important in some phases than others. Early adulthood is a time for acquiring material possessions both for pleasure and for status. Often the *'Unihipili* feels poor if it does not have the latest technology or the fanciest vehicle. Buying a certain type of home, living in an appropriate neighborhood, wearing a certain style of clothing, all indicate the preferences of the Selves for a particular lifestyle. Combining two lifestyles is another part of the adaptation process for newly weds. When the first child is born, the lifestyle changes again.

# *HUNA* TECHNIQUES FOR MASTERING EARLY ADULTHOOD SKILLS

> **Work: the ability to choose a fulfilling career.**

Career is a higher aspect of work. Career involves Purpose. This is a skill that is learned by both Selves with a mutual desire to succeed. The Selves often get stuck in jobs or careers that are not fulfilling or financially rewarding. These jobs are attempts to simply survive. The emotional stress and the intellectual inactivity make life difficult. The first step in learning this skill is to articulate your Purpose. The next step is to make a list of the talents and abilities of both your *'Unihipili* and *'Uhane*. Then list the desires and rewards of each Self. From Purpose, talents and abilities, and desires and rewards you choose a career field. Next list the positions you would like in the career. And finally you develop a plan how to get there. Sometimes the *'Unihipili* is fearful that the *'Uhane* will not take care of it in following the plan. It might disagree that night school may be too difficult. The *'Uhane* as guide and teacher of the *'Unihipili* must reassure it that the short and long range rewards are well worth the effort. An inner dialogue of reassurance and love repeated over and over is part of learning this skill.

> **Marriage or partnering: the ability to find a suitable person with whom to learn intimacy.**

Intimacy is first learned between the Selves. Intimacy is based on love, trust, understanding, acceptance, and tolerance. Being intimate with another person requires both Selves to practice these qualities. Being intimate with your partner is being comfortable with sharing who you are. Many people are attracted by physical magnetism. The *'Unihipili* of each person recognizes the qualities of the other and are energetically attracted. Sometimes the attraction is more on an intellectual level. For a successful marriage or partnership, the Selves must be attracted on the physical, emotional, intellectual, and spiritual level. For a marriage to be successful, each trinity of Selves must be integrated. How do we learn intimacy? We learn it by experimentation and repetition in a trusting environment. If you have emotions or thoughts concerning intimacy, you may need to master this skill. It begins with trust between the Selves. The practice involves the *'Uhane* keeping its word that it will follow through on its promises and taking loving care of the *'Unihipili*. The practice involves the *'Unihipili* controlling its feelings and allowing the *'Uhane* to make the decisions and sharing information with the *'Uhane*. It involves the realization of the spiritual aspects of the *'Aumakua* and the sharing of *mana* to create a loving environment for the Selves to experience intimacy. Then you practice with another person. Be objective and do not allow the *'Unihipili* to overwhelm the *'Uhane* with emotion. Pay attention to both emotion and logic in making partnering decisions.

> ## Child bearing and rearing: the ability to be good nurturers.

This skill is also based on the relationship between the Inner Selves. Nurturing skills of love, gentleness, support, encouragement, guidance, and teaching are all skills that the *'Uhane* and *'Unihipili* have been learning to this point. They are the inner skills practiced in the outer world. This skill is the parenting aspect of the *'Aumakua*, which the Selves imitate. The way in which the parents have been good nurturers form the basis of this skill. As young Selves we observe how our parents nurture and when we reach this phase, we put what we have observed into practice. However, some nurturing aspects of our parents may not be appropriate, and we can use our power to change those for our children. We can also study other ways of nurturing by reading books or observing other people who are good nurturers and follow their examples. We practice good nurturing by thinking before acting in situations where our own emotions spring up. We make a commitment to be loving nurturers.

# THE DEVELOPMENTAL PHASE OF MATURE ADULTHOOD

## THE INNER SELVES FROM THIRTY TO FIFTY YEARS

This is the time for the first house, family vacations, family fun and personal fulfillment. The Selves are now mentoring their own children, nurturing their growth, and enjoying the intimacy of family life. They are also reaching out to the greater community and expressing their Purpose in more meaningful ways. This phase of development is the time when one's career is established and covers the ages of thirty to fifty years. Towards the end of this phase, a person may decide to change careers or return to school.

The adult Selves in this phase are immersed in family life and with nurturing their own children. They are also enjoying the results of their hard work in chosen careers. In learning to organize their families they have learned the skills to organize other groups. This is the opportunity to reach out into the community and work for the betterment of society. Many Selves become leaders of youth groups, organizing social or religious activities. Others become involved in community organizations, clubs, or churches. The Selves volunteer their time and talents to support important social causes.

155

## Developmental Skills for Mature Adulthood

1. **Organize groups:** the ability to bring people together for a single purpose.

2. **Negotiate solutions:** the ability to work with both the intellectual and emotional minds.

3. **Personal commitments and empathy:** the ability to work with like-minded individuals and expand the higher emotional qualities.

4. **Social analysis:** the ability to observe and articulate situations, to detect and have insights.

5. **Transition:** the ability to move into a higher energy frequency.

To be a good negotiator, one must be aware of the intellectual and emotional aspects of problems. Many Selves have a natural ability to negotiate. This is a skill that all Selves need to master to work towards resolution of conflicts. Conflicts arise in the home, at work, and in the community. Mature adult Selves are intended to learn to negotiate for "win-win" solutions.

**Mature adults become masters of "win-win" negotiations.**

They now realize that we all must win or no one wins. This is a step forward from the competitive world of one winner and everyone else losers. Selves who practice "win-win" resolution in their negotiations are performing an important service to the world. Proper resolution brings the world closer to peace. The Older Selves can pass on this skill of negotiating to younger Selves and thereby increase the possibilities for world peace.

Through organizing and negotiating the Mature Adult Selves make personal connections with people of like-minds. These connections teach the Selves about empathy and relationships with a broader range of people outside the home and family. Empathy is a higher aspect of feeling. This is the age when the *'Uhane* assists the *'Unihipili* to move into the higher aspects of all feelings. The higher emotional aspects motivate both the *'Uhane* and *'Unihipili* to work towards improving the conditions of people who are not as fortunate or who need help.

With the ability to see the broader picture of life from the Mature Adult perspective and years of experience comes the ability to make social analyses and gain insights. The scope of knowledge of the Selves of this age moves outward to influence the community and the world. The Selves learn that what effects one part of the world effects all the other parts. Insights are gained through working with social issues. The Selves' Purpose expands to include a larger area of influence. Purpose begins to take a primary place.

A deeper understanding of sexual relationships is revealed during this phase. Sexual maturity includes the understanding that sexual energy is a form of prayer energy. The spiritual aspects of sex are explored. Mature Adult Selves are now more comfortable with their gender roles and more sensitive to the needs and desires of their partners. Each Self becomes better at expressing its uniqueness and creativity.

> **The "mid-life crisis" is about rediscovering Purpose.**

This is also the time for the "mid-life crisis." Towards the end of Mature Adulthood, a person begins to reflect on his or her life and relive decisions the Selves made that took them down one particular path instead of another. Women, who have devoted most of their adult life to bearing and raising children, suddenly find the nest empty and their *'Unihipili* feels lost. Men also feel this abandonment. This is one reason it is so important for the Selves to identify their Purpose earlier in life and not neglect it during the child rearing years. The Selves often realize that their chosen career has not satisfied their Purpose and they begin to look around for better modes of expression. The Selves might change careers at this time or seek higher education to make the change.

Towards the end of this phase, a woman faces what medical science has termed "menopause." This is a time when a woman's body moves away from the biological and emotional requirements of child bearing. Women cease to have "periods" and begin to experience "hot flashes." The medical community treats menopause as an illness and recommends all kinds of drug treatments. There is no medical evidence that hormonal therapy is beneficial to a woman. There are alternative and natural supplements that are just as effective. Accurate information, good nutrition, and regular exercise help a woman through the physical changes. How a woman handles the emotional changes depends on the integration of her Selves.

I prefer to call this time "*mana*-pause." A woman's energy, her *mana*, is being redirected and raised to a higher level. Her neurological circuits are changing from supporting child bearing energy to supporting wisdom energy. This process of shifting energy capacities involves the physical, emotional, mental and spiritual. Her *mana* is transforming from spiritual knowledge to spiritual action. I believe that women are changing on a cellular level and these "hot flashes" are really energy surges helping in this change. The *'Uhane* is reprogramming the neuro-circuits to

> **Menopause is really *Mana*-pause.**

handle this higher vibration of energy. The power surges are sent by the *'Unihipili* along these circuits to test and prepare them for a continuous flow. In order to have enough energy to reprogram these circuits, the *'Unihipili* is shutting down certain physical processes that will no longer be needed. As a woman approaches the age of 50, she comes fully into her feminine power. She has learned about her Selves and how to integrate them for powerful action. She can direct her *mana* and make effective prayers for healing. She is preparing for the next phase of Elderhood in which she becomes a receptor for energy and an active healer.

Men also go through *"**mana**-pause."* Biologically the changes are not quite as dramatic for men as they are for women. The emotional changes are just as

**Men also experience *"mana*-pause."**

difficult. The masculine reproductive energy is being redirected by the *'Unihipili* into the new neuro-circuits. The *mana* is raised to a higher frequency as men come into their full state of masculine wisdom. Men are preparing for the next phase of Elderhood in which they become healers and wise directors of energy.

Spirituality becomes a more important part of the lives of the Selves in this phase as the *mana* is being transformed to higher frequencies for both men and women. This uplifted or transformed *mana* is the next step toward the *mana-loa* of the *'Aumakua*. We need to learn the skills of using higher energy levels so the transition to the level of the *'Aumakua* is easier. We begin to use our higher *mana* in this phase. In the next phase of Elderhood, our developmental skill is to use our higher *mana* for healing and the good of all humankind.

**Spirituality becomes more important as we move towards the level of the *'Aumakua*.**

# *HUNA* TECHNIQUES FOR MASTERING MATURE ADULT SKILLS

> **Organize groups: the ability to bring people together for a single purpose.**

This skill is an organizational skill that includes the planning abilities of the *'Uhane* and the intuitive abilities of the *'Unihipili*. We learn this skill by observing those people who are good organizers and imitate them using our intuition. Begin by accepting a project to do for your favorite group. Start small and experiment with different types of organizational methods. Be clear on your responsibilities and the goals of the project. Celebrate your success. Take on increasingly difficult projects until you have mastered this skill.

> **Negotiate solutions: the ability to work with both the intellectual and emotional minds.**

This skill begins with negotiating solutions between your Inner Selves. Each mind has its own needs and goals. Learning how to meet these needs and goals in finding solutions results in integration. Each Self deserves to win. There are no winners and losers in finding solutions. The key is to find solutions that please both Selves. The same process is followed in negotiating solutions for others. The emotional and intellectual needs are considered and creative solutions are found. It takes time, understanding and persistence to learn this skill. Practice by negotiating first with your Inner Selves and then with increasingly difficult conflicts between other people.

> **Personal commitment and empathy: the ability to work with like-minded individuals and expand the higher emotional qualities.**

Personal commitment is an inner agreement between the Selves to work for a cause. If both Selves do not agree, it is not a commitment. Before committing to anything, you must first consult both Selves. We often commit on an emotional basis before we take time to think about it. Or we commit on an intellectual or logical basis because we think we should and don't take time to check our feelings. Empathy becomes stronger the more we commit ourselves. Empathy signals the ability of the *'Unihipili* to raise the quality of the emotions to their higher aspects. This skill requires the *'Uhane* to be informed of the higher aspects of emotions and to teach the *'Unihipili* how to raise its awareness. We learn this skill from observing the people we admire who can already do this. Then we practice.

**Social analysis: the ability to observe and articulate situations, to detect and have insights.**

This skill is built on the previous one. In order to understand social problems we must be able to observe the situation correctly and empathize with the people involved. We must also be able to put these observations and feelings into words that give a clear picture of what is happening. We use our knowledge and wisdom and listen to the intuition and inspiration of our *'Aumakua*, who sees the bigger picture. This skill requires the talents of all Three Selves and is learned through practice.

**Transition: the ability to move into a higher energy frequency.**

Both male and female Selves need this ability to progress to the next level of *'Aumakua*. It begins with the physical changes of mature adulthood and is completed in Elderhood. The *'Uhane* and the *'Unihipili* work together to reprogram the neuro-circuits to receive the higher energy by redirecting the reproductive energy to wisdom energy. We learn this skill by releasing our attachment to reproductive sexual energy and forming new attachments to wisdom or spiritual energy. It is part of the process of leaving behind what has been the focus of exploration in the physical world and moving back to our true focus on the spiritual world. We come to realize that the physical is a part of, and not separate from, the spiritual. We master this skill by practicing release. We support the *'Uhane* and *'Unihipili* in their work by maintaining a healthy diet, exercising regularly, and taking vitamin and mineral supplements to support cellular changes. We keep our emotional and intellectual minds active and balanced. We enjoy this transition period as we look forward to our new role as healer.

# THE DEVELOPMENTAL PHASE OF ELDERHOOD

# THE INNER SELVES AT FIFTY YEARS AND OLDER

All of the other phases of development have prepared the Selves for this final phase in the physical world. This is Elderhood, the time when we become <u>who we really are</u>. This is the time of wisdom, of spiritual maturity, of intellectual and emotional stability, of fulfillment of Purpose, and of healing. Elderhood begins at about 50 years of age and lasts until death. Elders are the connection between the generations, a connection that is vital to the survival of humanity.

Elders are the keepers of the wisdom, the guardians of the family history and teachings, a resource for important learning skills, experience, and knowledge. They are the wellspring of Spirit in a family's life. Elder's hold the "heart of the family." When Elders have a respected part in family life, they bring members closer, promote acceptance of diversity, appreciation and understanding of life. They encourage responsibility, self-respect, and active participation. They heal the body, mind, heart and spirit.

> **Elders hold the "heart of the family"**

161

Elderhood prepares us for our new level of consciousness. The 'Aumakua is not only the Divine Parent, but also the Divine Healer. The 'Aumakua heals body, mind, emotions, spirit, and circumstances. We explore new territory in Elderhood. We move into the realm of the Spirit while still existing in physical form. In ancestral cultures, Elderhood was achieved at a much earlier age. Today we continue to push Elderhood farther and farther into the future. We try to stay "young" as long as possible. We are not meant to be "young" forever, except in the sense of honoring and embracing the qualities of our younger Self, our 'Unihipili. We are meant to be whole and embrace our wisdom and continue to grow into our true Selves. If we avoid or postpone our transition into the phase of Elderhood, we hold back our own development. Our culture must change its focus from youth to wisdom. We need to look forward to becoming Elders.

This phase of development gives the Selves the opportunity for extensive introspection and self-evaluation, which fosters a sense of integrity and worth. It is a time for continued growth in areas that were impossible to explore earlier in life. It is the Golden Age of Life.

---

**Developmental Skills of Elderhood**

1. **Redirection of energy: the ability to use wisdom.**

2. **Acceptance of one's life: the ability to reflect and self-evaluate.**

3. **Spiritual fulfillment and healing: the ability to manifest and express Purpose.**

---

There are many new roles that Elder Selves take on during this phase of development. These new roles can be personal, social, political, or professional. Most Elder Selves retire at age 60-65 from careers and step into the volunteer world. Retirement doesn't mean we retire from life. Elders volunteer their services in new roles or continue as paid professional consultants and mentors. Many Elders join the Peace Corps to provide help to people in other countries. Other Elders, such as President and Mrs. Jimmy Carter, donate their time to build houses for underprivileged families. Still others join archaeological teams to help unearth and preserve the past. Some Elders enter politics and are elected to public office to work toward better government. All Elders become healers.

Elders are also grandparents and have been called "nature's gift to children." This describes the role of grandparents in the family. A grandparent is different from a parent. A grandparent has more patience and gives unconditional love to a child. As grandparents, Elder Selves give their grandchildren reassurance, comfort, and love from an older and wiser

| Elders are "nature's gift to children." |
| --- |

perspective. They give them laughter, fun, and a feeling of being special. Elder grandparents share all the unique talents and skills they have learned over the years with the next generation. Younger Selves need the Elder Selves, but often families live apart. It is up to the Elder Selves to keep the connection with their children and grandchildren. Elders are family healers.

Elders continue to take on more responsibilities in the modern world. Over 3 million grandparents are raising their grandchildren today. Parents have relinquished their family responsibilities for one reason or another. These Elder Selves deserve much respect, admiration and assistance. It is not easy to raise a second family during a phase that is the culmination of all the other phases.

Elderhood is a time for the Selves to enjoy and do all those things they have put off doing. This is a time for fun and play. Elders indulge in their favorite hobbies, such as golf or tennis. They go backpacking, hiking, swimming, sailing, hunting for fossils and artifacts, designing and sewing quilts, creating wonderful craft items and traveling the craft show circuit, or take up new hobbies. The opportunity to travel the

| Elderhood is a time for FUN. |
| --- |

country or the world is an activity the Elder Selves can now enjoy without worrying about family or work. This is meant to be a wonderful and fun time of life!

Elder Selves continue to lead healthy and productive lives. The great artist Pablo Picasso lived to be 91 years old. At age 79 he married his second wife and enjoyed 12 more years of married life. During the last 20 years of his life, he remained productive, energetic, and persistently continued to experiment with new art forms. Picasso fulfilled his Purpose and became a healer in the Arts.

## Elders can make a difference.

On Tuesday, February 29, 2000, "Granny D" Haddock ended her 3,000 mile walk across the United States on the steps of the Capitol Building in Washington, D. C. Granny D was concerned about campaign finance reform and decided to make a statement about her beliefs. Granny D is a fine example of a political healer. She turned 90 just before the completion of her journey. It took her 13 months to accomplish her goal and now she has more long range goals. She plans to continue to lobby for campaign reform wherever that may take her. There are many inspiring stories of people who have made a difference in this phase of their lives. This is the time for the Selves to make a difference, whether it is in making a 3,000 mile journey, volunteering in their community, or sharing their wisdom, experience and strength with their own families.

Accepting one's life and continuing to contribute to the greater whole is an important developmental skill for the Elderhood phase of development. If the Elder Selves have not yet lived their lives fully, it is not too late to get started. "Dying is not a sin: not living is." This is a time for reflection and introspection. It is the time to truly realize that our lives have been, and still are, worthwhile. We realize the lessons we have learned in this world and are preparing for our next stage of growth into spirit – death. Eventually we all pass again into the world of Spirit. How we have lived our lives makes the transition easier. The goal of the Elder Selves is to keep life exciting and challenging, even when we are "scared to death." This is the time for spiritual communion and deep faith. For *Huna* students, it is the time when the connection or channel to the 'Aumakua has been cleared and is completely open. This is the time for the Elder Selves to be the healers they are meant to be. All the other phases have prepared them for this golden moment of evolution.

> **"Dying is not a sin; not living is."**

> **To become a living healer, we must face the fear of dying.**

To become a living healer we must face the fear of dying. In *Huna* we know that death is the door through which we pass to reunite once more with our Divine Parent, our 'Aumakua. To others it means to reach Heaven or to pass again into oblivion. Whatever the belief, we must have faith in a higher power. In Elderhood our faith becomes our strength.

A few years ago, dying was treated as if it were "a separate realm of existence in American culture." America is still a death-denying society to some degree. In fact, in America birth and death have been banished to separate realms of existence, mysteriously taken care of for us by people in white coats in cold, sterile buildings away from the living. Birth and death belong to us as human beings. They are our rightful experiences.

Thanks to the work of great Elder healers, such as Elisabeth Kubler-Ross, death has returned to its rightful place in our lives. Hospice programs have returned dignity and honor to dying. In her book, *Death: the Final Stage of Growth*, Kubler-Ross comments about the Jewish law concerning death. This law states that the dying person must "be treated as he was always treated, as a complete person capable of conducting his own affairs and able to enter fully into human relations." The law also states that a "dying man is considered the same as a living man in every respect." The Selves are fully capable humans no matter what their state and as humans should be treated with respect and honor.

> # You are in charge of your life and your death.

Covering up grief and keeping people of all ages from experiencing death is a disservice to our humanity. This phase of development brings the death experience to many family members, relatives and friends. Elders can be spiritual healers to these loved ones as they ease their transition into Spirit. Death is also a time of reconciliation. In this last physical act, Elders bring families together to begin life anew.

By this time of life, the Selves have decided on a spiritual path. In some cultures, the years after marriage and child rearing are devoted solely to the spiritual path. Men and women give up all their worldly goods and retire to spiritual centers to pursue meditation and prayer. Elder Selves realize that the physical is a mere reflection of the spiritual. No matter what spiritual path a person chooses to follow, all paths go to only one place – HOME. We are born from Spirit and we return to Spirit. Spiritual fulfillment brings a sense of peace the Selves have not been able to experience until now. Through all the phases of development the Selves have learned that love is the common thread that connects us to one another. To express and experience that Divine Love is our ultimate goal.

The last developmental skill of this phase is fulfillment of Purpose. Through adolescence and adulthood Purpose has been a strong drive. Elder Selves now have more time and can devote themselves exclusively to fulfilling their Purpose. Purpose is the best expression of your life on earth. Through the fulfillment of Purpose we leave a legacy to our family and to the world. We live until we have finished the work we came to accomplish. This work can either be physical, emotional, mental or spiritual. Only the Selves know what that work is (our Purpose) and when it is finished. We are to finish our work and fulfill our Purpose with a flourish!

## Healing is the ultimate expression of our Purpose and our lives

165

# *HUNA* TECHNIQUES FOR MASTERING THE SKILLS OF ELDERHOOD

> **Redirection of energy to new roles: the ability to use wisdom.**

Role playing has always been a part of the life of the Selves. In this last phase of development the Selves take on new roles, the most important roles. The skill to fill the role of healer, Wise Elder, and grandparent requires the ability to use wisdom. Wisdom comes from all the experiences of life and from the many repetitions and experimentations of intellectual and emotional intelligence. Both heart and mind are used to choose thoughts, words, and actions. To become a healer, you must practice healing. Healing comes from the wisdom of your Inner Source. There is no right or wrong way to heal. Each healer has his or her own style. You have to trust your wisdom and intuition. Whatever your circumstances or lifestyle, you must practice healing the physical, emotional, mental, and spiritual dis-ease around you. Healing wisdom is needed by all beings in the physical world.

> **Acceptance of one's life: the ability to reflect and self-evaluate.**

The skill to reflect and self-evaluate is learned by reviewing one's life, the positive and negative aspects, the successes and failures, and the amount of loving influence you have had on the lives of others. Self-evaluation comes as you see your weaknesses and strengths. To learn this skill you must reflect and accept any hurts you have done to others, ask for forgiveness, and make amends. It is not always possible to accomplish this in person because people live too far away or have passed on into Spirit. However, you can ask for forgiveness through your *'Aumakua* and do good deeds in the name of the person you have hurt to make amends. In this process you completely clear away any last obstacles in the *aka* cord or connection to your *'Aumakua*. You clear away any remaining restrictions and allow the Selves to move again into Spirit.

Acceptance of one's life also means acceptance of one's death. You are the model, the example, to your children, families and friends, of meeting death fully conscious and with great dignity. This skill is learned by preparation. Talk to your children about death. It is through your example that they will understand that death is as much a part of life as birth. Make all arrangements for your death, burial, and memorial service well in advance. Prepare your estate and possessions to pass on to your heirs with the least amount of legal problems. Prepare and sign Living Wills that state your medical desires. In other words, be as responsible for your death as you have been responsible for your life. Let your children experience, through you, the healing moment of consciously dying in Spirit.

## Spiritual fulfillment and healing: the ability to manifest and express Purpose.

Our spiritual connection and the ability to use *mana* for healing complete the developmental skills. Healing is the art of bringing the spirit to the physical. Healing becomes a daily activity for the Elder Selves. It is a natural and self-fulfilling talent. The Selves become healers to everyone they meet. The healing energy flows outward from the heart of Spirit to those in need through the very body of the Elder Selves. The neuro-circuits are fully established in their new capacity to handle healing energy and they remain open continuously. To further enhance this skill, you visualize yourself as a channel for spiritual Light. Elders are the Light Bearers of the finest and brightest Light. Seize every opportunity to heal.

The manifesting of Purpose is the culmination of all our experiences on the earthly plane. We raise our consciousness to the highest possible level. It is our contribution to the good of humankind. This skill requires complete dedication to our Purpose in these last years of our physical life. We combine our emotional and intellectual minds with the Mind of Spirit to fulfill our Purpose. By fulfilling our Purpose we leave our legacy to the world.

# IN CONCLUSION

We learn to be good nurturers to our Inner Selves as we grow through the developmental phases of life. Each new skill we learn builds on the previous skills forming a network of support and knowledge for our existence. How we live and work with our Selves is more important than what we gain in material possessions. We measure success by how well we fulfill our Purpose.

As we learn to be good nurturers to our Inner Selves, we learn how to be good nurturers to each other. It is only by working together in love and healing that the human race can grow and evolve.

We are born into this world as explorers and leave as explorers to be born anew into a different world.

**May your journey of exploration lead you to WHOLENESS.**

# APPENDIX

## POEM TO NURTURE THE SELVES

This poem, written by an unknown author, gives the *'Uhane* good rules to follow in learning to be a guide and teacher to the *'Unihipili*. Copy this page and put it in a prominent place to remind you of what your want your Inner Selves to learn.

If a child lives with criticism, he learns to condemn.

If a child lives with security, he learns to have faith in himself.

If a child lives with hostility, he learns to fight.

If a child lives with acceptance, he learns to love.

If a child lives with fear, he learns to be apprehensive.

If a child lives with recognition, he learns to have a goal.

If a child lives with pity, he learns to be sorry for himself.

If a child lives with approval, he learns to like himself.

If a child lives with jealousy, he learns to feel guilty.

If a child lives with friendliness, he learns that the world is a nice place in which to live.

--Author Unknown

# BIBLIOGRAPHY

Acredolo, Linda and Goodwyn, Susan, *Baby Signs: How to Talk With Your Baby Before Your Baby Can Talk*, Contemporary Books, Chicago, IL, 1996.

Baker, Betta, "Helping Boys Become Men," AARP Bulletin, March 2000.

Bradshaw, John, *Homecoming: Reclaiming and Championing Your Inner Child*, Bantam Books, New York, NY 1990.

Cline, Foster and Fay, Jim, *Parenting with Love and Logic*, Pinon Press, Colorado Springs, CO 1990.

Covey, Stephen R., *The 7 Habits of Highly Effective Families*, Franklin Covey, New York, NY, 1997.

Csikszentmihalyi, Mihaly, *Finding Flow: The Psychology of Engagement with Everyday Life*, BasicBooks, New York, NY, 1997.

Eddy, Mary Baker, *Science and Health with Key to the Scriptures*, the Trustees under the Will of Mary Baker G. Eddy, Boston, MA, 1906 edition.

"Expectant Dads Change Too," The Denver Post, March 5, 2000.

Fillmore, Charles, *The Revealing Word*, Unity Books, Unity Village, MO, 1994 edition.

Gaskell, G.A., *Dictionary of All Scriptures and Myths*, Gramercy Books, New York, NY, 1991 edition.

Goleman, Daniel, *Emotional Intelligence*, Bantam Books, New York, NY, 1995.

"Got Cancer Killers?" Discover Magazine, June 1999.

Goodman, Robert B., Daws, Gavan and Sheiban, Ed, *The Hawaiians*, Island Heritage Ltd., Norfolk Island, Australia, 1970.

Harner, Michael, *The Way of the Shaman*, Harper & Row, San Francisco, CA, 1980, 1990.

Heffner, Elaine, *Mothering: The Emotional Experience of Motherhood After Freud and Feminism*, Doubleday & Company, Inc., Garden City, NY, 1978.

Hillman, James, *The Soul's Code: In Search of Character and Calling*, Random House, New York, NY, 1996.

Knight, Sirona and Starwyn, Michael, "New Ways of Communicating with Our Children," Magical Blend Magazine, January 2000 (Issue #68).

Krueger, Caryl Waller, *The Ten Commandments for Grandparents*, Abingdon Press, Nashville, TN, 1991.

Kubler-Ross, Elisabeth, *Death: the Final Stage of Growth*, Prentice-Hall, Inc., Englewood Cliffs, NJ, 1975.

Lee, Pali Jae and Willis, Koko, *Tales from the Night Rainbow*, Night Rainbow Publishing Co., Honolulu, HI 1990.

LeShan, Eda, *Grandparenting in a Changing World*, Newmarket Press, New York, NY, 1993.

Long, Max Freedom, *Growing Into Light*, DeVorss & Co., Los Angeles, CA, 1955.

Long, Max Freedom, *The Secret Science at Work*, DeVorss & Co., Marina del Rey, CA, 1953.

Murphy, Joseph, *The Amazing Laws of Cosmic Mind Power*, Parker Publishing Company, Inc., West Nyack, NY, 1965.

Newman, Barbara M. and Philip R., *Development Through Life: A Psychosocial Approach*, The Dorsey Press, Homewood, IL, 1975.

Poignant, Roslyn, *Oceanic Mythology*, The Hamlyn Publishing Group, England, 1967.

Porter, William, "The Phenomenon of 2 Minds in Tandem," The Denver Post, March 5, 2000.

Redfield, James, *The Celestine Prophecy*, Warner Books, Inc., New York, NY, 1997.

Redfield, James, *The Celestine Vision: Living the New Spiritual Awareness*, Warner Books, Inc., New York, NY, 1997.

Redfield, James, *The Secret of Shambhala: In Search of the Eleventh Insight*, Warner Books, Inc., New York, NY, 1999.

Russell, Peter, *Waking Up In Time: Finding Inner Peace In Times of Accelerating Change*, Origin Press, Inc., Novato, CA 1992, 1998.

Santo, Christine, "Can Baby Say 'downloadable file?" Access Magazine, Supplement to The Denver Post, February 27, 2000.

Sheehy, Gail, *The Silent Passage: Menopause*, Random House, New York, NY, 1992.

Smith, Anthony, *The Mind*, The Viking Press, New York, NY, 1984.

The Merriam-Webster Dictionary, Merriam-Webster, Inc., Springfield, MA, 1994.

Thevenin, Tine, *Mothering and Fathering: The Gender Differences in Child Rearing*, Avery Publishing Group, Inc., Garden City, NY, 1993.

Walters, G.T., *Follow Your Path*, Arize, Inc., Dallas, TX, 1986.

White, Burton L., *The First Three Years of Life*, Prentice Hall Press, New York, NY, 1985.

Whitrock, M.C., et al., *The Human Brain*, Prentice-Hall, Inc., Englewood Cliffs, NH, 1977.

Young, Samuel H., *Psychic Children*, Doubleday & Co., Inc., New York, NY, 1977.

http://www.cnn.com/HEALTH/9810/20/cord.blood/, Schiavone, Louise, "Umbilical Cord Blood Could Replace Blood Marrow Transplants."

Printed in the United States
107317LV00003B/35/A

9 780741 403988